Praise for *Double Your Price*

'This book is a must-read for anyone considering pricing for their products. With price often neglected in the rush for growth, Falzani highlights the long-term implications for cash, margins, profitability and ultimate value of the company, as well as providing a toolkit to address the thorny issue of pricing.'

Dr Andy Phillipps, co-founder, Booking.com

'One of the biggest challenges start-ups face is defining a route to market for innovative products and services. Understanding pricing lies at the heart of a successful commercialisation strategy, and this book provides an excellent basis for decision making. David Falzani takes the reader from the fundamentals of pricing all the way to the impact of subtle pricing changes on the success of the business. An essential read for entrepreneurs.'

Simon Barnes PhD, Managing Partner,
Tate & Lyle Ventures LP

'At last, a practical book on pricing. I enjoyed it so much I read it in one sitting, and I think it's essential reading for every start-up or large corporate alike.'

Henning von Spreckelsen, Management Board, Small
Business Charter and Fellow, Royal Academy of
Engineering

'This is a must-read for any business owner who wants to succeed and create a sustainable business. Professor Falzani is a regular contributor to our readers and this book reflects the wealth and depth of valued business insight and wisdom he has to share.'

Christina Lattimer, founder, People Development
Magazine

T0285190

DOUBLE YOUR PRICE

Pearson

At Pearson, we believe in learning – all kinds of learning for all kinds of people. Whether it's at home, in the classroom or in the workplace, learning is the key to improving our life chances.

That's why we're working with leading authors to bring you the latest thinking and best practices, so you can get better at the things that are important to you. You can learn on the page or on the move, and with content that's always crafted to help you understand quickly and apply what you've learned.

If you want to upgrade your personal skills or accelerate your career, become a more effective leader or more powerful communicator, discover new opportunities or simply find more inspiration, we can help you make progress in your work and life.

Every day our work helps learning flourish, and wherever learning flourishes, so do people.

To learn more, please visit us at **www.pearson.com**

The Financial Times

With a worldwide network of highly respected journalists, *The Financial Times* provides global business news, insightful opinion and expert analysis of business, finance and politics. With over 500 journalists reporting from 50 countries worldwide, our in-depth coverage of international news is objectively reported and analysed from an independent, global perspective.

To find out more, visit **www.ft.com**

David Falzani

DOUBLE YOUR PRICE

THE STRATEGY AND TACTICS OF SMART PRICING

With foreword by David Sainsbury,
Lord Sainsbury of Turville

Pearson

Harlow, England • London • New York • Boston • San Francisco • Toronto • Sydney
Dubai • Singapore • Hong Kong • Tokyo • Seoul • Taipei • New Delhi
Cape Town • São Paulo • Mexico City • Madrid • Amsterdam • Munich • Paris • Milan

PEARSON EDUCATION LIMITED
KAO Two
KAO Park
Harlow CM17 9NA
United Kingdom
Tel: +44 (0)1279 623623
Web: www.pearson.com

First edition published 2023 (print and electronic)

ISBN: 978-1-292-42634-1 (print)
      978-1-292-42635-8 (ePub)

British Library Cataloguing-in-Publication Data
A catalogue record for the print edition is available from the British Library

Library of Congress Cataloging-in-Publication Data
A catalog record for the print edition is available from the Library of Congress

10 9 8 7 6 5 4 3 2 1
27 26 25 24 23

Cover design by Two Associates

Print edition typeset in 9.5/13, Helvetica Neue LT W1G by Straive
Printed by Ashford Colour Press Ltd, Gosport

NOTE THAT ANY PAGE CROSS REFERENCES REFER TO THE PRINT EDITION

To my wife and soulmate Karen,
with all my love.

CONTENTS

Pearson's Commitment to Diversity, Equity and Inclusion

Pearson is dedicated to creating bias-free content that reflects the diversity, depth and breadth of all learners' lived experiences. We embrace the many dimensions of diversity including, but not limited to, race, ethnicity, gender, sex, sexual orientation, socioeconomic status, ability, age and religious or political beliefs.

Education is a powerful force for equity and change in our world. It has the potential to deliver opportunities that improve lives and enable economic mobility. As we work with authors to create content for every product and service, we acknowledge our responsibility to demonstrate inclusivity and incorporate diverse scholarship so that everyone can achieve their potential through learning. As the world's leading learning company, we have a duty to help drive change and live up to our purpose to help more people create a better life for themselves and to create a better world.

Our ambition is to purposefully contribute to a world where:

- Everyone has an equitable and lifelong opportunity to succeed through learning.
- Our educational products and services are inclusive and represent the rich diversity of learners.
- Our educational content accurately reflects the histories and lived experiences of the learners we serve.
- Our educational content prompts deeper discussions with students and motivates them to expand their own learning and worldview.

We are also committed to providing products that are fully accessible to all learners. As per Pearson's guidelines for accessible educational Web media, we test and retest the capabilities of our products against the highest standards for every release, following the WCAG guidelines in developing new products for copyright year 2022 and beyond. You can learn more about Pearson's commitment to accessibility at:

https://www.pearson.com/us/accessibility.html

ACKNOWLEDGEMENTS

I'd like to thank Simon Mosey, Paul Kirkham, Rob Carroll and all my colleagues at the Haydn Green Institute for Innovation and Entrepreneurship of Nottingham University Business School, Neil Robinson of Bulletin and the staff of Oxford University Saïd Business School's Goldman Sachs 10k SB programme. Thanks also to my good friend David Ciulla for his encouragement and support.

PUBLISHER'S ACKNOWLEDGEMENTS

PHOTO CREDITS

77 and 78 Shutterstock: Svetlana Foote/Shutterstock; 118 Shutterstock: Stephen Rees/Shutterstock.

TEXT CREDITS

19 Harvard Business Publishing: William A Sahlman: Innocent Drinks, Harvard Business School, 2004; 19 Fresh Trading Limited: Innocent Good All time report, 2019. Retrieved from https://www.innocentdrinks.co.uk/content/dam/innocent/gb/en/files/innocent-good-all-round-report-2019.pdf; 20 Centaur Media: Consumers' regard for Innocent crashes, By Marketing Week, 15 Apr 2009, https://www.marketingweek.com/consumers-regard-for-innocent-crashes/; 23 Tesco PLC: Tesco PLC; 64 and 228 Harvard Business School Publishing: Managing Price, Gaining Profit, Harvard Business Review; 65 McKinsey & Company: Alex Abdelnour and Walter Baker: Pricing: Distributors' most powerful value-creation lever, September 16, 2019; 78 Springer: Hermann Simon, (2015) Confessions of the Pricing Man, Springer; 86 The Chartered Institute of Marketing: Chartered Institute of Marketing; Help to Grow, HM Government, Small Business Charter; 107 Sage Publications: Gerstner, Eitan, 'Do high prices signal higher quality?' Journal of Marketing Research, 22(2), 209–215, 1985; 107 Sussex Publishers, LLC: Utpal M. Dholakia: When High Prices Attract Consumers and Low Prices Repel Them, February 5, 2018. Retrieved from www.psychologytoday.com/gb/blog/the-science-behind-behavior/201802/when-high-prices-attract-consumers-and-low-prices-repel-them; 110-111 Harvard Business School Publishing: Dorie Clark, Why You Should Charge Clients More Than You Think You're Worth, October 16, 2017; 111 Mind Advertising Ltd.: Stella Artois, https://www.adbrands.net/archive/uk/stella-artois-uk-p.htm; 112 Harvard Business Publishing: A.G. Lafley, Roger L. Martin, Jan W. Rivkin, and Nicolaj Siggelkow, Bringing Science to the Art of Strategy, September 2012. Retrieved from https://hbr.org/2012/09/bringing-science-to-the-art-of-strategy; 115 and

116 National Academy of Sciences: Marketing actions can modulate neural representations of experienced pleasantness. Hilke Plassmann, John O'Doherty, Baba Shiv, and Antonio Rangel. PNAS January 22, 2008 105 (3) 1050–1054; https://doi.org/10.1073/pnas.0706929105. https://www.pnas.org/content/105/3/1050.full; **126 Harvard Business Publishing:** Christof Binder and Dominique M. Hanssens, Why Strong Customer Relationships Trump Powerful Brands, April 14, 2015. Retrieved from https://hbr.org/2015/04/why-strong-customer-relationships-trump-powerful-brands?utm_source=Socialflow&utm_medium=Tweet&utm_campaign=Socialflow; **162 Penguin Random House:** Kahneman, Daniel, Thinking, Fast and Slow, Penguin, 2012; **177 Forbes Media LLC:** The World's most valuable brands, Forbes. Retrieved from https://www.forbes.com/the-worlds-most-valuable-brands/#df5daf119c0b.

ABOUT THE AUTHOR

David Falzani is an entrepreneur and Professor at Nottingham University. He has grown businesses by over 1,000% and trained over 2,000 companies, such as Oxford University's Goldman Sachs 10KSB, Rishi Sunak's Help to Grow and the Royal Academy of Engineering's LIF programme on growth initiatives. He has written 90+ articles and is also president of registered charity EIBF, whose MBA bursary recipients have created companies worth over £4.6 billion and 18,000 new jobs. He was made an MBE in the 2017 Queen's Birthday Honours list for services to enterprise and engineering.

FOREWORD

David Sainsbury, Lord Sainsbury of Turville

It is a great mistake to think that the pricing strategy of a business can be dealt with separately from the overall strategy of the business, and it is rarely the case that a low price is the right one for a business to adopt unless it has greater production efficiency or lower labour costs than its competitors.

The aim of most businesses must be to use technology and innovation, and an understanding of its customers, to create a competitive advantage for its products by making them more attractive to its customers. And commodity businesses, where it is not possible to gain a competitive advantage, should be avoided by a business unless climatic conditions or economies of scale enable it to have lower costs than its competitors.

Entrepreneurs setting up new businesses should always keep in mind the success of the Apple iPhone. The Apple iPhone makes huge amounts of value-added per capita for the company not because it is produced more cheaply than competing products, but because Apple has produced a product which in terms of the services it provides, its ease of use and the quality of its design makes it highly desirable to consumers who are, therefore, prepared to pay a higher price for it. And by a constant process of innovation and its amazing engineering skills, Apple is always able to stay ahead of its competitors.

All these points are of particular importance for companies which have to compete with companies in newly developed countries such as Taiwan, Singapore and South Korea. These countries can now manufacture goods as well as we can, and they still have lower wages. Instead of seeking to lower their costs and prices in a 'race to the bottom', businesses in the Western world should seek in 'a race to the top' to increase their rate of innovation and in that way create the new, high knowledge-intensive products of the future for which consumers are prepared to pay a premium.

In this excellent down-to-earth book on pricing, David Falzani shows how companies can make good pricing decisions which enable them to be profitable, reinvest and grow, and just as importantly how to avoid the mistakes made by many new entrepreneurs. It should be read by all those who want to set up new companies and grow profitably in the highly competitive global markets of today.

CHAPTER 1

WHY YOU SHOULD READ THIS BOOK

This book is about the strategy and tactics of smart pricing. It's for anyone who wishes to understand how pricing works and how to avoid common mistakes, including those due to cognitive bias. Along the way you will discover insights, tools and actionable guidance on how to set and manage prices; when and how to harness higher prices in a beneficial way. This will allow you to understand how to create a value-seeking entrepreneurial culture in your organisation, how to talk about pricing strategy with others and how to get them on board.

This book is therefore for business managers, business owners, students and entrepreneurs. More broadly, it's for those who wish to grow a business – whether a new one or an established one – and are interested in how this can be helped by smart pricing. Done correctly, smart pricing can also help avoid the time-consuming and expensive process of raising new investment, such as pursuing bank loans or selling shares to investors, which are otherwise often required for growth.

My principal aim in writing this book is to help businesses avoid a critical error that is seen again and again while working with companies, both large and small. That error is underpricing or pricing incorrectly. It's one of the most common failings encountered in early stage enterprises; it's also a mistake many long-established businesses make, and it's a mistake that hugely damages any business's chances of real success. There's often a 'sweet spot' for any price, but whilst prices can be too high or too low, being too low tends to be far more common. In considering how any given price is perceived, companies also often underestimate how important the 'framing' of pricing is.

Price is one of the most important factors in determining whether any growing firm survives and thrives, yet the perils of underpricing remain massively unappreciated. This enduring blind spot doesn't just represent a major threat to an individual growth business; by extension, it also jeopardises a country's broader societal and economic health.

Revisiting pricing, and applying smart pricing, is therefore a worthy exercise for businesses, both large and small.

In any country, start-ups and small and medium enterprises (SMEs) are usually the innovators in their markets. They represent the high-growth, cutting-edge concerns that are most likely to increase national productivity, keep the economy in good shape and solve many of the problems we all face. In the UK they comprise 99 per cent of businesses, 60 per cent of jobs in the private sector and more than 50 per cent of annual turnover. In the USA, 30 million SMEs account for nearly two-thirds of new private sector jobs[1] and half of all US jobs.

Start-ups and SMEs are also key drivers of innovation for large corporations, which acquire them to access innovative solutions and new technologies.

By training a spotlight on price in this book, I aim to contribute to the support available to both small and large corporations by explaining and correcting the cognitive bias that too often compels the owners of start-ups and managers of large businesses to focus on doing things cheaply rather than better. As we'll see, 'better' is by far the preferable route – while 'cheaper' frequently ends in disaster.

By the end of this book, you will have a useful grasp of why price is actually both valuable and strategic. You'll appreciate why it's something to be actively pursued and why it's essential to any enterprise's ability to survive and thrive. You'll understand why the common practice of setting prices just once, or perhaps annually, is both flawed and, from a business perspective, potentially fatal.

This book will answer these questions:

- How much should we charge for our product or service?
- How much are our customers willing to pay?
- If we increase our price, will we lose customers?
- How can setting prices help us cover our costs?
- What are the benefits of a pricing strategy?
- Will increasing or decreasing prices help my business succeed?

WHAT THIS BOOK ISN'T

Given the title of this book, it's vital to stress from the outset that raising prices in this context isn't about encouraging profiteering or 'price gouging'. Such an approach is neither laudable nor sustainable, and we should dismiss all thoughts of it immediately.

In these pages at least, raising prices is instead about generating economic surpluses for reinvesting in product[2] development and encouraging innovation. It's about providing superior employee training and paying higher salaries to well-motivated, capable staff. It's about enhancing capabilities and reducing staff turnover. It's about delivering superior value to customers and creating a happier, more skilled, more productive workforce. Ultimately, it's about finding ways to make a business better for all its stakeholders.

HOW THIS BOOK WORKS

This book presents many options, techniques and different approaches. It also contains many examples and exercises to help you apply these principles to your own company, including a collated workbook for you to refer to at the end of the book.

Pricing sits within *sales and marketing,* which is a topic area that's rich but extremely diverse. There are many industry-specific approaches and norms, which is why I've tried to take a broad view and offer a range of insights and solutions around the importance of pricing in general.

Some of these insights and solutions will be applicable to your company, and some won't. I'll be your guide through this variety of approaches so that you can *cherry-pick* and find a handful of golden nuggets that will transform your understanding of how price works for you and for your organisation, unleashing tremendous value in the process.

The book therefore explains the tools and techniques that companies use today in setting price, as well as some of the dirty tricks they sometimes employ to extract higher prices from customers and consumers. These are explained in the book and you can decide how to best use this information – for example, some readers may wish to raise their own awareness in order to protect themselves as a consumer.

We'll start our analysis in Chapter 2 with the curse of underpricing and by considering why the phenomenon is so widespread in what we might call 'high-growth businesses'. This is the *catch-all term* that will usually be used henceforth to describe entrepreneurial firms of all sizes, whether start-ups, SMEs or growing companies, all of which have similar issues with regard to pricing. In Chapter 3 we'll see it also includes larger, more stable, organisations – who are often no less at risk.

In Chapter 4 we'll review the traditional theory on price, which was first developed in US universities in the 1930s, and reflect on why it doesn't meet the demands of today's high-growth businesses. We'll then discover why price is so important for growth in Chapter 5 and how it links to supporting positive cash flow.

Developing good pricing practices, in Chapter 6 we'll examine why price should almost never be 'cost plus' – despite the enduring popularity of this approach – and then move on to understand how pricing *should* work. We'll reflect on how the relationship between price and value is changing in Chapters 7 and 8 and explore how to unlock growth with respect to the reinvestment rates that high-growth businesses can generate.

The final portion of the book is concerned with how to move forward. Chapter 9 poses a tantalising question – *'Is there a way you can double your price?'* – and the following three chapters offer insights into key cognitive biases, such as framing and priming, as well as strategies for price increases and suggestions for a new form of value management.

All this should leave you in little or no doubt that treating price as something to be kept to a minimum can often prove erroneous, if not catastrophic. Although it may sound paradoxical, the fact is that almost every successful high-growth business I've been involved with has had a very generous budget furnished by a smart pricing strategy. A low-price culture isn't necessarily a low-*risk* culture.

CHAPTER 2

WHY UNDERPRICING IS A KEY BUSINESS ERROR

U nderpricing is one of the most common problems encountered when training, mentoring or coaching early stage businesses. It's also a common problem seen when consulting for large corporations, and some high-profile corporate collapses will be mentioned in Chapter 3, where tiny changes to price could have made a substantial difference to the outcomes.

So, what is underpricing? Underpricing is where a company routinely sells something for a price that is materially lower than the price that could have been achieved.

It's therefore where a company has taken a decision to set a price, but that price point is lower than it needs to be. This could be by even 1 or 2 per cent. This sounds small but, as we'll come on to see, it's a material amount and has a much larger effect on the bottom line than many expect. The underpricing company is essentially leaving money on the table and not receiving the full economic reward that it deserves.

Setting prices is often something companies dislike doing in any case. While some firms are painfully aware that they're underpricing, others simply haven't considered the issue – even when their prices are far too low to support their needs. This book is not claiming it's true for all businesses – there are exceptions where price management is virtually irrelevant – but almost all companies are, at best, not maximising the role that price has to play and, at worst, endangering their future success by underpricing.

It's often a simple case of not demanding a fair price for a decent product or service. The reason this is a 'problem' is that these businesses don't realise that in not charging a sufficiently high price they're severely limiting their prospects of making a living and enabling growth. Underpricing reduces profits, which in turn reduces a company's ability to invest in the future, reward its staff and improve its offering.

Some 60 per cent of new businesses fail within three years,[1] with lack of profit margin and cash flow a major contributing factor to this alarming rate. Even for those that stagger on, low prices and consequent low margins can stifle growth – keeping small companies small or suppressing growth, suffocating potential and undermining sustainability of even the largest corporations.

WHAT COMPANIES USUALLY SAY

Here are some typical comments from companies lamenting their inability to set and raise prices.

'I'M WORRIED THAT IF I HAVE A HIGHER PRICE, I WON'T WIN THE BUSINESS.'

This company is expressing a belief that customers won't buy from it if its price is any higher. The implication is that customers are highly cost sensitive and actively choose lower-priced offers. The next chapter will talk about price elasticity of demand and how buying behaviour can change with price, but it's also quite possible that the company in question has an underlying lack of confidence in its value proposition. In other words, it isn't truly convinced that its product or offering is valuable to customers and/or sufficiently different to what others are offering to give it a compelling and significant offering in the face of the customer decision-making process.

'WE'VE GONE TO THE TROUBLE OF GETTING TO THE FINAL STAGE OF THE PROCESS AND DON'T WANT TO FAIL NOW.'

Here the worry is that so much time and energy – and therefore cost – has gone into establishing a dialogue that raising prices could somehow scupper all the effort and lose the investment made. The concept of a sunk cost (please see the paragraph below for an explanation) has perhaps not been considered.

Do you encounter similar concerns in your business? If there's a track record of spending time and effort (and money too) in establishing a business development opportunity, is there a sense of pressure to bring things to a successful close? Where does this pressure come from and are there things you can do to mitigate it?

A useful concept to consider here is the idea of a sunk cost. A sunk cost is one that has been incurred and can't be recovered. As such it shouldn't influence a decision about the future. Past investment decisions (including any past mistakes) should be irrelevant in arriving at choices about what lies ahead, otherwise the risk is 'throwing good money after bad'. Therefore, a new decision should be based on its own merits, not according to what has been already spent. An example of a sunk cost in popular culture is the so-called 'Concorde fallacy', whereby the governments of the UK and France continued to invest in Concorde because of the high levels of past investment instead of simply writing off the costs and moving on. Concorde was never a commercial success.

In the quotation above there's also a missing context of how many dialogues are available – if one is underway does that mean that there are not many others to pursue? Losing one bad deal can be the cost of winning a suitable proportion of the other opportunities. Nonetheless, at the time of the quote, the implied pressure of the sunk cost can be formidable.

'WE'RE IN A TENDER-BASED BUSINESS. THE CUSTOMER CHOOSES ON PRICE.'

An invitation to tender can constitute a special case. There are procurement processes that simply choose on price and select the cheapest option – a reverse auction is one example – but these aren't usual. Most tenders are assessed according to a matrix of different criteria, such as delivery performance and quality metrics, with price only a component of the overall selection (Chapter 5 highlights some research on this). This is, of course, also true for many purchase decisions outside of a tendering process.

In addition, many customers relate price to quality. Being too cheap may therefore suggest lower standards. It's no coincidence that most leaders in their market sectors charge a high price.

'WE'RE ALREADY MORE EXPENSIVE THAN OUR COMPETITORS.'

This business assumes not only that its data and statement are correct – which they may or may not be – but that it knows who its competitors are, and is able to compare the relative strengths of the customer value proposition and value drivers rather than just monetary figures. Sometimes, as we'll explore later, the real competitors are selling at double the reference price or more.

The quotation also assumes that customers are rational and able to make accurate comparisons. The overwhelming evidence shows this not to be the case.

WHOSE INTERESTS ARE BEING REPRESENTED?

In many cases it's also worth asking in whose interests a buyer (or supplier[2]) is acting and what those interests might be. There are two interesting questions that highlight this point:

1. If you wish to negotiate a long-term relationship with a supplier, would you rather deal with the owner or an employee?

   What is your view on this and why?

The second question is slightly different:

2. If you wish to negotiate a lower price with a supplier, would you rather deal with the owner or an employee?

   Again, what is your view on this and why?

With the first question, the interests in establishing a long-term relationship are clearly more likely to be with the owner of the business. A long-term relationship could potentially deliver value over a long period of time. An employee, by contrast, may only be in a particular role and/or with a particular employer for a much shorter time than the typical business owner. The business owner therefore has the greater interest in a longer-term engagement.

With the second question regarding price, any reduction in price essentially comes directly out of the business owner's pocket: a reduction in price will lead to a reduction in profits, which would ultimately have gone to the owner. By contrast, an employee is usually rewarded with a salary that is fixed, so giving a discount has no economic effect on them. Assuming that the employee is authorised to deal with price, and this is often the case, then they have far less 'skin in the game' and are more likely to be disposed to a price discount.

More generally, what can this tell us from a setting-of-price perspective? Asking the question of 'whose interests are at stake, and what are those interests?' gives insights on how price sensitive a buyer may be, and can help frame follow-on questions to which answers can be pursued. A buyer who's a business owner may wish to 'get good value' – whatever that might mean to them: it may include a monetary portion, but may well include something else. A buyer who's an employee may be more concerned with career progression, gaining kudos or simply not getting fired. Also, if a budget already exists, and this is often the case with public money, then any sum up to the budget limit could be equally acceptable to an employee, particularly if there's no bonus from coming in far below the budget.

EXERCISE

Whose interests are being represented?

For your company's customers, in whose interests is the buyer acting? And what are those interests?

▶

1. *List your top five customers, or a key customer from each market that you serve.*

2. *For each entry, ask yourself the following questions:*

   a. *Who are the principal decision makers?*

      i. *Who are they in the organisation?*

      ii. *How many of them are involved?*

      iii. *What is each of their roles in decision making – do they specify, recommend or authorise?*

   b. *Whose interests do they represent?*

      i. *Are they acting for their own interests, for their boss's, for their company's, for their family's?*

   c. *What are those interests?*

      i. *What do they wish for?*

      ii. *What expectations do they have?*

      iii. *What are their underlying motivations?*

      iv. *What time period do they serve?*

      v. *What can you do to better serve these interests?*

      vi. *What are the consequences if the relationship fails?*

   d. *What are your interests?*

      i. *Which of your interests are shared with, or conflict with, the customer's?*

      ii. *Can you influence their interests and/or alternatives?*

      iii. *Are you able to somehow creatively build on shared interests or bridge conflicting interests?*

      iv. *Given all of the above, how can you otherwise better align your interests with the buyer's?*

Guidance: The exercise targets a particular customer audience and seeks to expose the underlying traits that drive a customer's decision making – separating the individual's needs from external factors, such as an employer's needs, in the case of an employee carrying out the purchasing, or their personal or family's needs for a private individual. In doing the exercise, it's helpful to start with the answers that you can readily supply. Any questions you are unable

> *to initially answer can be tackled later, either by some discrete research or as you accumulate more knowledge. As ever, the more information you have about the context within which someone is making buying decisions, the more able you are to align your interests and achieve superior outcomes.*

THE USUAL REASONS FOR KEEPING PRICING LOW

The most common response companies give when asked to explain why they feel they can't raise their prices is that they're very keen to bring in a sale. There's an underlying belief that a higher price will make this less likely. There's sometimes even a sense of desperation.

As mentioned in Chapter 1, a company usually tries to keep its prices low for one, or several, of the following reasons:

- A lack of confidence in its value proposition and its ability to bring in higher-priced business
- A fear of not having enough sales and throughput to meet overheads and fixed costs, such as paying salaries
- Price has been set some time ago and is not actively reviewed.

Let's look at each of these in more detail:

LACK OF CONFIDENCE IN THE VALUE PROPOSITION

One reason for this mindset can be disappointment at not winning business. Past experience of not securing the desired custom can cloud future decisions, leading a firm to believe low pricing is the only means of 'sweetening the deal' and generating sales.

Another cause can be customer complaints over expense. Unfortunately, some customers – and particularly some *types* of customer – consistently moan that prices are too high. Such gripes are really just natural behaviour. We might even say it's the job of a certain type of customer to grumble about prices. Other customers, by contrast, purchase without comment.

A key point here is that customer feedback is always context specific. We all want customers who love our products and services, but the fact is that many have learnt that asking for price discounts really does work – as a consequence of which there might be something of a game to be played. As I'm fond of saying, the easiest way to introduce a discount is to introduce a price rise first. I recommend using data to analyse such situations – for example, what evidence is there that customers have acted differently if denied a discount?

Also, sometimes a customer's request for a discount can be a welcome opportunity to on-sell and up-sell another aspect of an offering. An on-sell involves selling an additional item as part of the same transaction, while an up-sell involves selling a higher-end item, or larger item, in place of the item originally under consideration. By finding something of value to a customer – ideally, without a large marginal cost to you – you can maintain your margins and possibly increase the overall invoice amount. If you can increase the average transaction value and marginal profitability increases, then you are positively increasing the price.

Transaction value

The idea of average transaction value is useful. If an interaction with a customer has a certain cost associated with it, then any increase in the amount spent in the transaction essentially increases the money that goes towards profits. The increased spend for the transaction increases the average price per transaction.

It's worth repeating that the value proposition, fundamentally, encapsulates what you do that customers value, and which is in some way different – or differentiated – from the competition. It includes the relationship you have with the customer and the trust and confidence you generate. Making the effort to think about, and then develop, a strong value proposition is a key element of business success – one that should be complemented by other aspects of your offering, such as credit terms and promotional strategies.

FEAR OF INSUFFICIENT SALES

This mindset has its roots in desperation to generate enough sales to cover costs. In tandem it stems from an associated belief in price elasticity of demand and a rational market – i.e. a conviction that a lower price will increase transactions by augmenting the chances of customers saying 'yes' and reaching for their credit cards.

In reality the customers who help a company grow are actually likely to feel quite the opposite. They tend to be sceptical about low-priced offerings and instead look for interesting features. Meanwhile, by simply buying whatever happens to be cheap, 'bottom-feeding', disloyal, price-shopping customers thwart a firm's attempts to grow.

It's important to remember that we can segment customers in any market or product category by various criteria, including segmenting by their cost sensitivity. Premium customers who are willing to pay a higher price are obviously far more profitable and attractive from a business perspective, while those at the other end of the spectrum – those intensely cost sensitive and with no loyalty to any particular provider – hold comparatively little appeal.

So, what is meant by 'price elasticity of demand'? The concept is covered in more detail in the next chapter, but it's one with which we're all familiar with as a result of our own experiences as consumers. We all know shops hold 'sales' or discount campaigns to sell their wares and we all know these efforts are usually intended to shift products or services that have previously attracted scant interest.

Widely applied in much of the management theory developed for major corporations in the US in the 1930s, the idea of price elasticity of demand is best applied to mass markets and big companies with high turnovers and very large numbers of customers. Crucially it's not so relevant to early stage or high-growth businesses where an innovative entrepreneur can find new approaches and novel ways of doing things, not to real-world and usually 'imperfect' markets – which are very different to the idealised 'perfect markets' that traditional economists theorise over.

By way of further warning for high-growth businesses, let's briefly consider the phenomenon of seasonal discounts or seasonal sales. They effectively penalise those customers who have paid full price, and they also encourage people to wait for discounts – thus undermining a company's hopes of success. This isn't the stuff of sustainability as far start-ups and SMEs are concerned.

And what about the 'rational market'? Cases where a CEO succumbs to desperation and reduces prices in a bid to be competitive often hinge on an underlying belief about what can or can't be changed, what's fixed and structural and what's possible – all of which is usually a sign that some form of cognitive bias is holding sway.

This potentially destructive spiral is frequently grounded in faith in a rational world – one in which people and companies use perfect information to make logical decisions and mistakes and emotional involvement simply doesn't exist. There's a wealth of evidence to show there's actually no such world – which is unfortunate for some entrepreneurs but fortunate for others, because irrationality, as we'll see later, is a source of significant business opportunity.

The sale sits at the top of the P&L – we can 'fix it' lower down

There's also sometimes a belief that as long as business is brought in – i.e. a sale is achieved – any profitability issues can be managed later on, further down the Profit & Loss (P&L) statement. The aim in such instances is to manage down costs and thereby deliver a healthy profit. This view is misguided, both because it assumes costs can be actively managed or changed – they often can't – and because the effort required to manage down costs in a company focused on business development will be displaced by the effort required to keep building a sales pipeline. For large companies, anecdotal evidence suggests that mangers spend more time on trying to manage down costs than on anything else.

The self-reinforcing negative cycle and death spiral

A company that becomes a budget operator with low prices will very likely experience a lack of profits generated by sales. This means it won't have the resources to reinvest in getting better at what it does. The value proposition will suffer, and the firm will become less valuable to customers and less competitive. This will lead to further price reductions, and the cycle will accelerate towards eventual bankruptcy if nothing is changed.

This form of downward spiral is surprisingly easy to fall into. Many businesses carry out actions without fully understanding the self-reinforcing nature of those actions. In this particular case decisions lead to, and reinforce, further decisions that send a company down a particular pathway without fully understanding the ramifications of that pathway. Extreme cases of this behaviour are sometimes known as a death spiral, whereby a business reacting to a negative circumstance makes a series of decisions which ultimately make the circumstance worse and lead to an ever more severe spiral into failure.

A simple example of this might be a company that has kept prices very low and so doesn't have the profits to reinvest into customer support and service, which in turn means it can't attract or retain customers, who then eventually go elsewhere to make their purchases. In response to this and to attract trade, the company further reduces the prices, reinforcing the negative cycle that will lead to its inevitable bankruptcy.

PRICE HAS BEEN SET SOME TIME AGO AND IS NOT ACTIVELY REVIEWED

The third usual reason for not increasing prices is, in some ways, a mixture of the previous reasons. Price is sometimes seen as something either immaterial, immutable or irrelevant. In all of these cases the importance and frequency with which price is considered is inappropriate and dangerous for growing organisations.

In some cases it may be that there is a feeling that price is the responsibility of someone else in the organisation to review and/or set. It could be that, in actual fact, it is no one's responsibility.

It could be that price is reviewed, but this is only done perhaps once a year, or whenever a new product cycle begins, which could be every three or four years. After this, there is no active checking and reviewing of the pricing points or their context.

There is, therefore, often a sense of price being something fixed, something that we have to live with, rather than an opportunity to generate value.

Without smart pricing, in all these cases, at best, there's a lost opportunity to build value and improve the organisation's position, and at worst, a danger of undermining the organisation's future.

WHAT IS COGNITIVE BIAS?

I've mentioned that some of these assumptions are cognitive biases, but what exactly *is* a cognitive bias? In short, it's a belief or feeling that leads to poor decision making. It might be due to the emotional baggage we all carry around; it might be a consequence of naivety or inexperience; it might even have its roots in our evolutionary history, as an aid to arriving at decisions with speed. Even though they have a disproportionately large effect on what we do, cognitive biases routinely go unrecognised and unacknowledged.

SOME EXAMPLES OF COGNITIVE BIAS

Confirmation bias occurs when people select friends, information sources and data that reflect what they already believe. This means their choices are only ever likely to reinforce their existing opinions, with little or no chance of a logical and evidence-based review of these convictions. For example, a disturbing trend in politics is the increasing preference for online media that bolster users' own viewpoints leading to a degradation of open debate, greater polarisation of perspectives and more closed-mindedness. This is also popularly termed an *echo chamber.*

Anchoring is an important bias. It's often used in business negotiations where the first offer 'put on the table' anchors the ensuing exchange. It's so called because it's very difficult to move or drag once it's in place, just like a ship's anchor. It means the first piece of information is treated as disproportionately significant.

Imagine, for example, a classic bargaining scenario: buying a rug in a market where there are no price labels. You ask how much the rug is, the seller gives you a figure, which is the starting point – the anchor; you go back and forth and eventually part once the deal has been done or has come to nothing. A good example of everyday anchoring is the role of price tags on consumer goods in a department store or used cars in a showroom. Another notable example is the use of price points in coffee shops to influence decision making (as we'll see in Chapter 9).

Availability bias means we tend to overly rely on whatever piece of information is at hand rather than seek a statistically instructive set of data. An example is where recent memories of media stories on aircraft accidents or robberies lead to a judgement that such events are far more common than they really are.

All three of these biases are common in business decision making, and especially in the context around the potential for actually changing prices as well as the setting of the actual price itself. Later in the book we will delve into cognitive biases in more detail.

MOST HIGH-GROWTH COMPANIES CHARGE PREMIUM PRICES

It's essential to understand the role of higher prices in bringing success. There's much evidence to show most high-growth businesses, rather than being low priced, actually charge *premium* prices. By now this shouldn't be totally surprising as we've already touched on the importance of prices in supporting profits, which in turn drive cash generation, which in turn promotes the business stability and reinvestment needed in staff and products and processes in order to grow.

Let's look at some examples of high-growth companies.

INNOCENT DRINKS

Innocent Drinks' sales grew by 27,900% between 2000 and 2007.

Innocent was founded by three University of Cambridge graduates in 1998. They started selling 'smoothie' style drinks, and the company grew rapidly. Innocent's unique selling proposition, its competitive advantage if you prefer, was that its smoothies were made by crushing whole fruits, as opposed to using concentrates, which was the approach favoured by the existing market leader.

The company went through a period of spectacular growth, with high demand for its products. This can be seen in Figure 2.1.

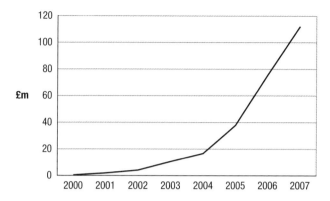

Figure 2.1 Innocent Drinks sales, 2000–2007[3]

With strong messaging around health and sustainability, Innocent was able to sell its smoothies at a premium price in comparison to both existing smoothie competitors and to fruit juices.

Innocent rapidly became the UK's fastest growing food company, with sales going from zero to over £10 million in just four years. This achievement was undoubtedly assisted by having prices significantly higher than the competition and other established offerings. This helped the business achieve its considerable growth by providing healthy gross profit margins and allowing reinvestment in the business.

Innocent's designer produced a 250ml bottle design, which the company would sell at the same price as the main smoothie competitor's 330ml bottle. This already suggests a significant price premium per unit volume of 32% over smoothie competitors. However, compared to other fruit juices:

'The price per millilitre of a smoothie could be five times the price per millilitre of Tropicana orange juice.'[4]

As one of the founders explained:

'In retrospect, the price may have actually helped our growth by sending a signal that our drinks were something different.'[5]

It's clear that a premium price model was not only present, but that the premium pricing also contributed to the considerable success. Although Innocent's subsequent acquisition by Coca-Cola makes comparisons more difficult now, this price-premium position still appears to be the case today (see Figure 2.2).

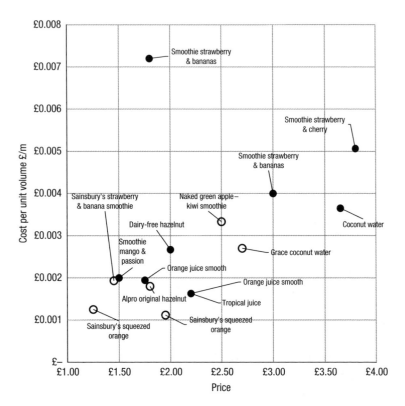

Figure 2.2 Position of Innocent's products compared to the competitors

Note: Innocent's products are shown with solid circles. Products higher up or further to the right-hand side reflect premium pricing

Whether driven by competitors' response to Innocent's success, or by other interest, the media did report on the company's higher prices:

> 'Innocent has come under fire for the premium price of its offering in the past.'[6]

It's worth noting that customers obviously found huge value in Innocent's proposition and were not troubled by the prices – we know this from the spectacular sales growth.

APPLE

Apple's sales grew by 3,159% between 2000 and 2019 (see Figure 2.3). The company's brand, designs and reputation allow it to charge premium prices for its products while also incentivising customers to stay with the business across its product range.

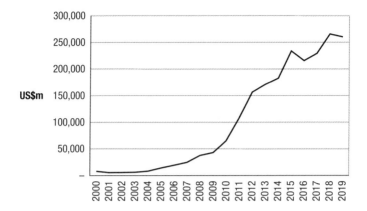

Figure 2.3 Apple sales, 2000–2019

Although direct comparisons are difficult, by way of illustration of the firm's pricing philosophy, a simple Apple phone power lead might retail for 400% of the price of an Android phone manufacturer's comparable product. Similarly, in 2015 the average price of an Android smartphone was said to be nearly three times lower than the average cost of an Apple iPhone.[7]

Apple is so good at convincing customers that its products are worth paying extra for, that the company has reportedly had up to $250,000,000,000 (that's $250 billion) of cash in the bank and is the first publicly traded US business to reach a market capitalisation – total value of shares – of over $2 trillion. This is all due to margins, driven by higher prices.

AMAZON

Amazon is another company that has grown spectacularly over the past 20 years. It sells products on a B2C (business-to-consumer) basis via its website and also has Amazon Web Services, one of the largest B2B (business-to-business) providers of web hosting. Its sales increased by an astounding 28,049,900% between 1995 and 2019, during which period the average annual growth rate was 69% (see Figure 2.4).

Amazon actively prices according to market rates for a whole raft of products. In general, analysis has shown it's 10–15% more expensive than its main competitors[8] – despite its origins as a seller of discounted books. This price premium may have helped it generate profits that it has reinvested to develop a value proposition based on a fair price and outstanding delivery and service. Customers routinely state they use the company because of efficiency and convenience factors rather than because they can't find cheaper alternatives.

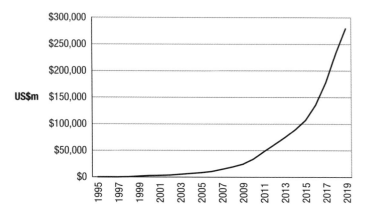

Figure 2.4 Amazon sales, 1995–2019

FACEBOOK (META)

Facebook (recently renamed Meta) grew its sales by over 7,000% between 2009 and 2018, whilst the average annual growth rate was 61%. It's principally a B2B enterprise since its customers are advertisers (as opposed to its users, who are consumers targeted by the advertising). Facebook uses its market position and data to command premium advertising prices.

Although it's somewhat difficult to make straightforward comparisons between advertising prices, one strong form of evidence of a premium pricing model is in the reported profit margins. Facebook has high and growing net profit margins of 37%, 39% and 40% in the last three years, as seen in Figure 2.5. Few businesses of any kind can boast those sorts of percentage

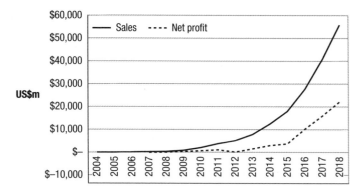

Figure 2.5 Facebook sales and net profits, 2004–2018

margins, particularly businesses quite so large. This is strong evidence for a premium model that has powered Facebook's growth.

TESCO

Tesco is the #1 supermarket in the UK at the time of writing and the third biggest in the world by gross revenues. Its sales grew by 288% between 1998 and 2019 (see Figure 2.6).[9]

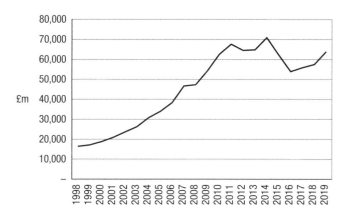

Figure 2.6 Tesco sales, 1998–2019

A recent study by *The Grocer* demonstrated that the company charges a 13% higher price on average than its next competitor.[10] This is an industry where claiming a low price for products is regarded as a critical success factor, yet millions of customers prefer Tesco in spite of its higher prices. Buyers are clearly looking beyond a low-cost culture and finding other value in what Tesco does.

LIVING ON A SHOESTRING

There are, of course, instances where selling at a lower price can be a successful strategy. Yet these are almost invariably based on a fundamental or even structural cost advantage that allows great profit margins.

The best example of this is the emergence of a new technology that has fundamental advantages over existing solutions. The jet engine, for example, offered far lower costs per passenger per mile compared to piston engines, effectively replacing the latter for long-distance air travel; cheap gas largely replaced expensive oil for heating buildings; electric lights replaced gas lights; the Model T replaced the horse and so on.

When these fundamental advantages don't exist, all too commonly, entrepreneurs use low pricing to try to win business – thus placing themselves in a position of not making a fair living. Many are willing to 'suffer' in this way in the belief – or hope – that the ordeal will be short term. They create a business with marginal viability of a proposition. Another way of thinking about this is a company which does not have a sustainable competitive advantage or compelling value proposition.

Such companies are difficult to scale and grow. Entrepreneurs who, in effect, make *themselves* the cost advantage are saying they're willing to earn less and be *leaner* than their competitors in order to compete. This sounds like a reasonable approach until, as we'll see in later chapters, we take into account the importance of having healthy profits to reinvest back into product development, technology, service offerings and staff welfare.

There's an interesting question we'll explore in Chapter 3: Would you prefer to have a £100 million business with a £1 million profit or a £10 million business with a £1 million profit? The first has a margin of 1%, the second 10%. The 10%-margin company is likely to be less lean and less financially rigid and will increase profits more quickly in line with any rise in sales.

HOW CAN YOU IDENTIFY IF YOU ARE UNDERPRICING?

There are some questions you can ask yourself to see if you are underpricing, to see if you are 'leaving money on the table' when it comes to framing and setting price:

- Do you feel that your business has enough cash to meet your growth needs?
- Are your profits higher than your competitors, particularly at the gross margin level? (See Chapter 12 to learn how to do this analysis.)
- Have you carried out a frank comparison of features, benefits and prices to your competitors?
- Are you feeling relaxed about how critical the price you set is in the process of acquiring your sales?
- Are you able to recruit enough high-quality staff to support the business processes that you would wish to have?
- Are you able to be more generous with investments and employee benefits than other companies in your sector?
- Are your IT and infrastructure fully up to date and well resourced?

■ Do you review your prices often, including in the last month?

■ Do you understand what messages your customers receive about your value proposition and how you compare to competitors?

■ Do you understand how customers come to recognise how high or low your price is compared to other options they have?

If you have answered 'no' to a majority of these questions, then there's a good chance that you are underpricing.

USING SINGLE USE ECONOMICS TO CHECK THE BUSINESS MODEL

Another useful technique in analysing your profitability and offering some insights on whether your price is too low, is to look at single use economics.

One form of single use economics is the single case model for a particular business, i.e. for a single customer, how much money do you receive compared to the amount of cost that you expend in providing the product or service?

If the costs in delivering the service are higher than the income received (which is partially set by the price), then the value proposition is loss making and will ultimately fail.

This analysis is in contrast with what many companies do (and is particularly common with innovative businesses), which is to aggregate the profitability analysis in a five-year growth forecast.

This forecast can show sales, costs and forecast profits without truly understanding the underlying economics. This is because the timing of the associated sales and costs under cash accounting are not correctly matched. In other words, if a sale in a time period in the P&L is recorded, but the costs directly associated with the sale are not recognised (or paid) until the following period, then the profitability in the first period is flattered – it is shown deceptively high. The costs may be actually higher than the sale amount, and thereby the proposition may be fundamentally loss making, but the mismatched P&L forecast can be positive.

There are many ongoing businesses that have these economics, and they can succeed only as long as the P&L grows. As soon as the business stutters, or there is an economic downturn, they usually fail rapidly.

Therefore, a five-year forecast can deceive, since it can appear very positive despite the business not having a fundamentally positive business model. Single use economics provides a route to prevent this error. The analysis can also take into account both the situation today, and then the situation at some point in the future when the solution matures, or economies of scale come into play.

So far, we've examined the dangers of underpricing and some of the reasons why businesses set their prices too low. Next, we'll review some basic pricing theory before moving on to prove the importance of price to success.

CHAPTER SUMMARY

- Underpricing destroys businesses: it's a major factor in the demise or stalling of many companies both large and small companies.

- Companies often feel reluctant to review pricing. Understanding key interests in sales transactions can help change this view.

- Evidence suggests successful, high-growth companies charge *premium* prices.

- Premium prices allow reinvestment in operations to build sustainable market positions.

- Businesses minimise their prices due to lack of confidence in their value proposition or fear of losing sales and/or not covering overheads.

- Cognitive biases are at play and make it harder for a company to make decisions to scale up, reinvest and grow.

Things to consider

Underpricing

If you suspect you are underpricing, why do you think you are doing this?

e.g. lack of confidence, fear of insufficient sales, price is immutable

Cognitive bias

Which cognitive biases are you subject to?

e.g. confirmation bias, anchoring, availability bias

Interests

In whose interests are your buyers acting?

What are those interests?

Chapter exercise

Whose interests are being represented?

CHAPTER 3

THE ENORMOUS INFLUENCE OF PRICE – WHAT IS PRICING?

P rice is often viewed as something that has to be 'managed down' or minimised in order to deliver acceptable value to customers and be competitive in the marketplace. As such, it's often a source of guilt for the owners of start-ups and managers of larger businesses.

This sense of guilt is misplaced. It's a consequence of cognitive bias. Price shouldn't be viewed as a reason for self-reproach; it should be viewed as an opportunity to generate high rates of return, enhance a business's offering and increase customer value.

It's the relationship between price and value that's particularly misunderstood. It might be obvious that greater customer value should lead to greater price, but the fact that price is a driver of value in its own right is routinely overlooked. The surprising reality, as we'll see, is that customers appreciate opportunities to, and often wish to, pay more. Taken within context, this insight offers businesses an opportunity they may otherwise not be aware of, and can help offset some of the management bias.

So why do businesses try to keep their prices low? Let's recap: it's usually due either to a lack of confidence in a value proposition, or to a fear of not having enough sales and throughput to meet overheads and fixed costs or price simply hasn't been revisited often enough.

The first reason indicates that a company doubts its products or services. The second reason assumes a simplistic price elasticity of demand – i.e. that having a lower price will increase the number of sales transactions and the chances of a particular customer saying 'yes'. Both are highly problematic, and in due course we'll explore the faulty reasoning behind them (as well as the issue of not revisiting price often enough) – and, crucially, examine the potential solutions.

Recognition of these truths is a powerful step towards smart pricing and enabling future growth. By way of illustration, look at the major success stories of recent years. Start-ups, high-growth entities, internet 'unicorns' – almost all have had a premium price model relative to their peers, while very few have been low-price leaders. The fact is that higher prices are more likely to allow a company to grow each year, and without requiring high levels of external investment.

LARGE CORPORATIONS MAKE THE SAME ERROR

It's not just smaller companies that make the mistake of underpricing. It can also be found in large and mature businesses, particularly where there's transparency of price data in the market – in other words, easy availability of competitors' prices to draw comparisons against – which can encourage damaging price wars.

The past few years have seen several high-profile corporate collapses, one of which claimed the travel firm Thomas Cook. The company ceased trading in 2019, leaving 21,000 staff and 600,000 stranded customers in dire straits. In its final year it had losses after tax of £163 million.

Assuming for a moment that profit is a good indicator of business success and continuation, it's interesting to wonder how much of a price rise would have allowed Thomas Cook to reach break-even in its last year. The answer is that a 1.7% increase in average transaction value – or price – would have done the trick.[1]

Since 1.7% is a relatively small number, is it reasonable to think the board of directors and senior managers couldn't find a way to implement such a modest uplift? I think it unlikely. The fact is that large corporations and boards of directors don't revisit the role of pricing frequently enough and instead see it as an occasional task to be delegated. Price is seldom regarded as something good, something progressive, something to be actively managed, reviewed and controlled. Directors often delegate the responsibility to mid-level management, even though it's a topic whose influence and potential should qualify it as a matter of the utmost importance.

UK retailer BHS offers a further illustration. It went into receivership (or administration), unable to continue trading, putting 11,000 jobs at risk and with pension fund deficits of £571 million. In its annual accounts for 2013 it showed a loss of £887,000 at the gross profit level. What kind of increase would have produced a break-even in this instance?

The answer is that a rise in average transaction value – or price – of just 0.13% would have allowed BHS to break even at the gross profit level.[2] Things got a little worse the following year, the final year of normal trading, but even then, an increase 0.84% would have been sufficient.

Large corporations and their accounting rules are complex, of course, and I'm not suggesting all roads to failure are related to price. Governance and accrual accounting principles allow judgements to be made in reporting, which in turn influence the registered levels of profit; a lack of innovation, a poor value proposition, high levels of debt interest payments and cash-flow problems might all also be amongst the factors.

Nonetheless, the question still stands: are the directors of these companies aware of the influence that price has on their businesses and are they spending sufficient time looking at it? Moreover, are they actively using the latest understanding around pricing to ensure the success, or even continuation, of their enterprises?

TRANSFER PRICING

By contrast, one area of pricing that large corporations are clearly active in, and have become somewhat notorious for, is related to transfer pricing. Transfer pricing is a mechanism by which multinational companies can decide in which jurisdiction they pay tax, and therefore how much tax they pay, subject to the applicable laws.

The principle behind this process is that a multinational can move products through sister companies in different countries and set the prices that each company charges to each other company (the 'transfer price'). In this way, the profit margin reported by each company in each country is influenced by the internal transfer price, which the company can set in order to achieve certain tax objectives.

Transfer pricing is, perhaps understandably, seen in a very negative light by many, including the popular press.

THE QUEST FOR VOLUME

Many entrepreneurs, managers and owners of high-growth businesses focus on sales volume. They understand that increasing the number of units sold improves overall revenue. In essence, their belief is that growing a sales base grows a company.

Often, however, this ethos is either mistaken or irrelevant. Profitability and cash flow, not sales volume, are usually far more likely to drive a firm's survival, fitness and, ultimately, valuation. This is why I habitually ask business executives the following question:

Which company would you prefer to have?

a. *A £100m sales company with profits of £1m*

 or

b. *A £10m sales company with profits of £1m*

Ask yourself which you would rather own. Or, which you would prefer to manage. It's a really great question – one that offers insights into the 'soul' of entrepreneurs and managers. Let's compare the two candidates again:

Company	A	B
Sales	£100m	£10m
Profit	£1m	£1m
Profit margin	1%	10%
	Prefer?	Prefer?

Both have the same profit. Company A has tenfold the sales of B. All things being equal, there's little doubt that A will be the far bigger entity in terms of employees, infrastructure, physical assets and so on – but it's also likely to be far bigger in terms of complexity and therefore in terms of risk. By contrast, B is likely to be smaller, less complex and less risky.

There is, though, another way of thinking about risk, which is to consider profit margins. I would argue that A's 1% profit margin is far more sensitive to disruption caused by economic shocks and competitive pressures than B's 10% profit margin.

That said, it's not always so simple. Some entrepreneurs might wish to provide jobs for a large sales force, which could steer them towards A; similarly, some managers might wish to have substantial empires under their control or boast about the size of their 'top-line' sales, which would again make A the more appealing choice. There's no right or wrong answer per se. It boils down to what resonates with, and is deemed important by, an individual manager.

A high-growth business I worked with in 2020 remarked:

'. . . Your question, "Would you prefer to have a £100m business with a £1m profit or a £10m business with a £1m profit?", has had a profound impact on our approach and has informed a change in emphasis within our business. Instead of going for revenue growth, we're aiming for solid profit for the benefit of the company and, specifically, for our hardworking team. . .'

This is an interesting comment. I've been involved with companies with 1% net margins and companies with 10% net margins, and I can unequivocally state that the latter are usually far nicer places! They tend to have happier, healthier staff; they offer better perks, such as company days out and training; they boast more relaxed environments and more progressive cultures; they're more creative and fulfilling; they usually have better-paid employees and they're more productive.

I'm often impressed by how much CEOs and founders care about their employees. Many see their workers as members of an extended family. Higher pricing supports this sentiment and opens the door to a better workplace.

Equally, it's worth noting that the valuation of companies that are actively trading is usually calculated on the strength of profit-after-tax figures (or sometimes by cash flow). Top-line sales are very seldom used. Profits are required because companies need to cover their costs, and covering costs is key to sustainability.

Of course, an excessive focus on top-line sales figures is in many ways perfectly natural. It's easy to understand why it's popular. Sales are relatively easy to measure, whereas the complexity of measuring and allocating costs makes profits hard to calculate; and sales figures are more or less instantly available from a transaction register or bank account, whereas profit figures are usually delayed – sometimes by many months. N.B. An even worse behaviour in many large corporations is an almost maniacal focus on market share, where increases or decreases in market share are seen as being of paramount importance – this highly competitive perspective further distances the company from profits and from customer value generation.

In the end, though, companies need profits to survive, to generate cash flow, to reinvest and to grow. There's little point in having high sales in the absence of profit, because that's just a fast way to get miserable and go out of business – as we'll see over the following chapters.

CHAPTER SUMMARY

- Price is most often regarded as something that should be minimised to deliver acceptable competitiveness.

- Price setting is often revisited only occasionally.

- For many high-profile corporate failures, a very small increase in average transaction value could have led to profit break-even.

- Underpricing is a costly error amongst businesses of all sizes.

- The 'which company' question is most useful to diagnose the priorities of the business leader.

Things to consider

'Soul' insights

Which company would you prefer to have?
a. A £100m sales company with profits of £1m? Why? / Why not?
or
b. A £10m sales company with profits of £1m? Why? / Why not?

Potential?

Which companies (or brands) that you interact with do you think have growth potential? What role does price have in this?

CHAPTER 4

PRICING 101: THE BASICS – PLUS SOME SURPRISES

P rice, and the setting of prices is one of the '4 Ps' of classical marketing theory.[1] However, the setting of prices is no simple thing. Being both operational and strategic, setting price correctly requires an understanding of both the internal company environment and the highly complex external environment of competitors, customer perceptions of value and the decision-making processes used to make purchases.

It's therefore well worth taking a look at traditional basic pricing theory to help us understand where some of our preconceptions concerning pricing come from. As was mentioned earlier, much of this microeconomic theory was developed many years ago for large corporations and 'big businesses' of the time to understand more about the markets and challenges that they faced, which is all quite different to the challenges of the high-growth business today.[2]

PRICE ELASTICITY

Price elasticity of demand is a principle in economic theory. It says that as the price of a product changes, the demand for it will change too. If the price goes lower, the higher the demand for it will be, and vice versa, according to the principles of supply and demand.[3]

In other words, the lower price will encourage more people to buy, or a higher price will put them off. The degree to which this is said to be true depends on the angle of the line and is usually dependent on the specific market characteristics. It's possible to measure the angle of this line, the price elasticity of demand, and in the charts you can see examples of different angles from 'highly elastic' to 'slightly elastic'.

HIGHLY ELASTIC DEMAND

As you can see in Figure 4.1, markets with high levels of price elasticity of demand mean that if there's a change in price (a) there's a relatively much larger change in demand, or quantity sold (b). This means that the market is highly sensitive to changes in price.

SLIGHTLY ELASTIC DEMAND

Markets with just a slight price elasticity of demand mean that the same change in price (a) here this time creates a much smaller change in demand (b). In Figure 4.2 you can see the different steepness of the slope compared to Figure 4.1.

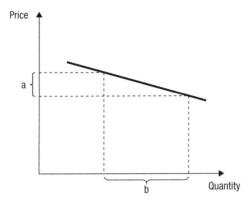

Figure 4.1 A high price elasticity of demand curve: a change in price creates a relatively much larger change in demand

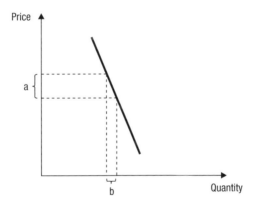

Figure 4.2 A slight price elasticity of demand curve: a change in price creates a much smaller change in demand

PERFECT INELASTIC DEMAND

In this case, markets where there is zero (or inelastic) price sensitivity of demand, means that the demand remains the same irrespective of the price point. The price may go up or down but the demand is still the same (see Figure 4.3). This may seem like a somewhat extreme case, but it's certainly true where products are so highly differentiated that they are not seen as 'substitutes', and also where demand is simply fixed for other reasons.

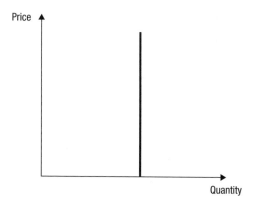

Figure 4.3 A zero price elasticity (inelastic) of demand curve: the demand remains the same irrespective of the price point

An oft-used example of this might be a person stranded in the desert dying of thirst being offered a bottle of water to buy. The exact price is irrelevant in the sense that they would be willing to pay any price they can afford to not die of thirst.

THE ASSUMPTION OF RATIONAL MARKET PLAYERS

However, ideas such as price elasticity often assume that the market is rational, which is to say making rational (or economically logical) decisions, and that information is available to the market which allows it to make efficient decisions. However, I would argue that these assumptions are often not appropriate for our target audience of high-growth companies (which tend to target new opportunities or bring new entrepreneurial perspectives to opportunities).

Again, many of these economic theories are based on 1930s' 'big corporation' management theory which was developed to explain behaviours in enormous commodity markets, such as grain and steel production. Today's high-growth companies have products and services that are hard to compare 'like for like'. This is because they have high levels of innovation or are very well differentiated, making comparisons difficult. This fact alone makes the price elasticity concept inappropriate. Worse, the concept can underpin incorrect thinking about the way companies price their offerings.

This thinking is the mistake high-growth companies can sometimes make in believing that in keeping their prices low they are more likely to bring in business and achieve sales. More importantly, it ignores the question, 'Which types of customer does a company want?' Does it want those who are most cost conscious or those who are looking for something more special and are willing to pay more for it?

PRODUCT LIFE CYCLES AND PRICING

Product life cycles are present all around us and form a part of classical marketing theory. In general, whenever a new product or product category is created it goes through the phases of the life cycle. There are four distinct phases – there's the introduction phase, followed by growth, then maturity and then decline (see Figure 4.4).

In the introduction phase, a new offering starts. Sales are initially minimal although they then start to grow. Because of this low level, the profits will be negative – the sales are not high enough to cover the costs incurred. For innovators, this portion of the life cycle can be the most critical, since this is where customers have to be matched to the value proposition. Finding early adopters is usually key, as these are the customers who are more open to trying new things, and their engagement can help build a 'beachhead' to the much larger sized markets in the later phases.

In the growth phase, sales grow strongly and, somewhere along the way, the product becomes profitable and then profits grow strongly in line with sales growth.

In the maturity stage, profits start to plateau and then decline. This is often due to the entry of competitors and the resulting pressures that this introduces in terms of pricing pressures and/or increased costs to serve the market (such as increased promotional costs). Sales also then start to plateau. This indicates that the product is perhaps reaching a later stage

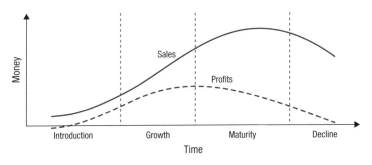

Figure 4.4 The product life cycle

of its life cycle where growth is either muted, or zero, or perhaps slightly negative. This could be because the market has reached its maximum potential.

In the final phase, decline, sales drop off and profits also decline back towards break-even, or even to loss-making levels. The category is clearly in decline – it could be due to the introduction of a new parallel product category, which will eventually supersede and replace this one. In effect, you can imagine multiple product life cycles leading to one another as new products and improvements are created.

From a price perspective there are two broad entry strategies for a new product: price skimming or penetration pricing. In price skimming, a high price is maintained with a view of having few but higher margin sales to a focused audience – for example, to early adopters. By contrast, penetration pricing is intended to set a lower price in order to serve a much larger portion of the potential market (the market penetration is greater).

Price skimming tends to be applicable where products are well differentiated (or very different), there are high levels of desire in the market, price is less important to the market, it's difficult to duplicate the product and a fast return on investment is required. Penetration pricing supports the opposites in each dimension. Often, many product categories start with high prices (price skimming) but then later prices drop (penetration pricing) and the products become universally popular – consumer electronic products are usually a good example of this.

PRICE AND PERFORMANCE

One of the most basic ideas when buying goods or services is that the more you pay, the better performance you get. In other words, if someone wants a higher quality or more capable product or service, they will have to pay more for it. A Rolls Royce car costs more than a Ford. A Concorde jetliner costs more than a Cessna, and so on. This is partly because we tend to believe that a higher quality product will cost more to produce, hence a higher price is charged. Also, a higher performance product will give us more value, so it's fair that we pay more for it. These are usually the underlying assumptions.

So, as price increases, so does performance. If you want more performance, you pay a higher price. This basic relationship is shown in Figure 4.5.

However, what happens if there is no difference in the delivery cost for higher performance? For example, moving a passenger up from an

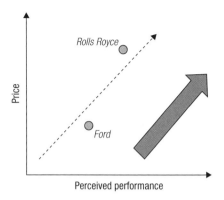

Figure 4.5 Price is proportional to performance

economy seat to an empty business class seat on a long-haul flight. What's the extra cost? Actually, it's zero or close to zero. It doesn't change the fuel cost, nor the staff cost, and the meals are already on board, to be used or discarded, anyway.

Another example: what about getting a premium satellite or streaming video channel added to an existing service plan? The cost increase for the supplier to do this is almost zero. Apart from a tiny amount for the labour at the customer service centre to press a button to switch it on, the extra ongoing operating cost for someone to receive the signal is zero.

Similarly, what's the difference in costs incurred between a designer piece of clothing and a mid-level one? If you remove the brand label, the garments are often made to the same range of shapes, in the same factories by the same people on the same machines and using the same stock of fabrics. Unless the fabric or design is particularly unusual, then the garments and costs are basically identical.

Once you start to ask these sorts of questions it rapidly becomes clear that there are many examples where prices are higher irrespective of whether the costs of provision are proportionally higher or not. Please keep this in mind as we proceed through the chapter.

A MULTIPRICE-POINT STRATEGY

It's also important to consider multiprice points for products. Many product categories have an array of price points. These price points can be aligned to the performance of the product, whereby the higher the performance of the product the higher the price.

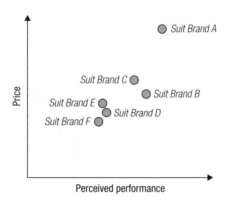

Figure 4.6 The basic relationship between performance and price

An example of this basic relationship is shown in Figure 4.6 illustrating a variety of competing clothing brands selling a range of men's suits at different price points. You can see that the presumably higher performing, or premium, brands are more expensive, perhaps with a suggestion of higher quality, whilst the less premium, lower quality garments are at lower price points.

You can see the distribution of price points goes upwards in the expected roughly linear fashion, in this case at an angle of about 45 degrees, although the angle can vary widely.

Again, our intuition tells us that this general distribution must be correct. In our experiences as consumers, we are used to making trade-offs between things we can afford and those that we cannot justify paying the extra for. In the belief that we are rational decision makers, we believe we look for 'value for money'. We look for the 'sweet spot' where we believe we get the optimal solution for our needs. Either that, or some people report that they buy the *stuff* that 'feels right' and 'feels good' up to the point that they can comfortably afford. The more money they have, the higher this point is.

THE PRODUCT IS THE SAME, EXCEPT FOR PACKAGING AND BRAND

However, would it surprise you to discover that, actually, the products in Figure 4.6 are often actually *the same*? That they are physically *identical*?

It's quite common. In many categories, the competitive products can be placed on a scatter diagram with differing prices as above, but are actually *identical* in terms of their functional ingredients, or, if you prefer, their manufacturing. The only things that are different in these cases are the packaging and the brand.

Good examples are as diverse as cosmetics, painkillers and washing machine detergent but there are many, many others. The only functional difference between these competing products in each category is the way they are physically presented via packaging, physical design and branding. Also, sometimes in the way they are sold. Looking at the active ingredients of such products, they are actually *functionally identical,* often made in the same factory by the same workers.

This means, as you can see in Figure 4.7, although many products may appear to offer different performance, and occupy many price points, they are actually the same.

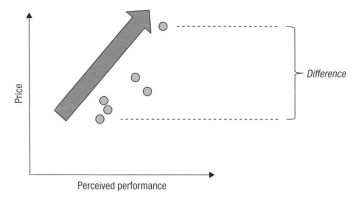

Figure 4.7 Despite the price differences, are the products essentially identical?

Perceived performance can be a very subjective thing. And that's the point. When it's hard to establish differences in performance in an analytical laboratory setting, then more arbitrary factors, such as emotional content, come into play – and these are very much leveraged by brand messaging and packaging.

WATER – THE ULTIMATE CONSUMER GOOD

An even better example is water. Bottled water is sometimes called the ultimate consumer good, and with good reason.

If you look at a bottle of water selling at £1 and a similar-sized bottle selling at £4, what's the difference between them? What's the active ingredient in both? It's water, which is the molecule H_2O. It's an oxygen atom with bonds to two hydrogen atoms. The water molecule in all cases is identical,

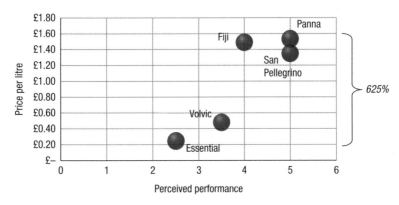

Figure 4.8 Water: price and performance

it's H_2O. And yet you can compare different brands of still mineral water and see that the price difference range is more than an astonishing 600% (see Figure 4.8).

Again, the only material difference between these competing products is the way they are physically presented via the packaging's design and the branding that goes with it. The H_2O molecules are identical. As a source of hydration for the consumer, they are functionally identical.

This simple truth holds good for many luxury goods too. They are often made in the same factories by the same workers with the same materials. This goes back to premium 'designer' clothing brands as a good example: Ask yourself next time you see a premium clothing offer what the actual difference between it and a regular piece of clothing is. People might be led to believe, usually through implied messages in advertising, that the materials are higher quality, the construction is more precise. However, what *proof* do you have that there is a real difference? The reality is that they are often the same, apart from the designer label.

As mentioned above, perceived performance – the horizontal axis in Figure 4.8 – is a subjective thing unless you can physically measure it, so for the following charts, rather than trying and estimating it, I've adopted a slightly different chart, but hopefully you will still get the idea.[4]

WASHING POWDER

Washing powder manufacturers spend a lot of advertising time and money convincing you that they are very different from each other and offer vastly improved levels of performance. However, a quick look at the ingredients listing shows that they are broadly very similar, if not identical. A simple

Figure 4.9 Washing powder: variety of price per kilo and price point - a unit price range of over 500%

sanity check, or thought experiment, for this would be to ask, if the last 20 years of advertising telling us all about the 'new and improved' XYZ brand is true, then why after 20 years of these apparent vast leaps forward, are the washing products basically the same as they were?

In Figure 4.9 each dot is a washing powder from the same retailer. The horizontal axis shows the different price points that are on this supermarket's shelf. The vertical axis shows the price per unit of weight (£ per kg). You can see that at any given price point there is a wide variety of costs per kilo. People are therefore paying a big difference for essentially the same thing. The price range is up to 575%.

Similarly, many manufacturers actually publish 'cost per wash' figures, which makes the comparison even easier. Remember, these washing products all do the same thing. The price range is £0.15–£0.44 per wash, a ratio of up to 290%.

SALT

Salt is another great example of something basic, that is very straight forward, and yet is sold at very different prices. The active ingredient of salt is sodium chloride, which has the chemical formula $NaCl$. Here again, you can see the differences in prices asked (see Figure 4.10). Each dot is a packet of kitchen salt sold by the same retailer. Along the horizontal axis you can again see the different price points that are present on the store shelf. However, you can see on the vertical axis the very different price per kilo that salt is being sold at – consumers are paying a price range of 2,000% for essentially the same thing.

Figure 4.10 Salt: variety of price per kilo and price points, showing a 2,000% variation for the same thing

CRISPS

Most people enjoy potato crisps (or potato 'chips' in North America). To provide a little variety, Figure 4.11 is a little different: the horizontal axis here shows the packet size, or weight in grams, of over 100 crisp products. The vertical axis represents the price per unit weight for that product. You could argue that there is more difference between competitors in this category due to quality of flavourings and so on, but nonetheless, you can see once again the difference of price per 'unit' for crisps approaches 400%.

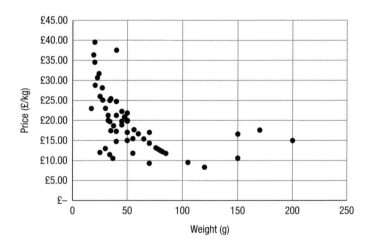

Figure 4.11 Crisps: price per kg for various packet sizes

PARACETAMOL PAINKILLERS

Figure 4.12 is a scattergram for 500mg paracetamol tablets. In all cases, the product is paracetamol in 500mg tablets made to the same medical standards for consumption by consumers. They are therefore identical apart from the packaging, the tablet shape and/or colour and the brand name. They are even sold in the same shops side by side, and yet the more expensive ones clearly prosper – they can, of course, afford the expensive advertising thanks to the higher prices.

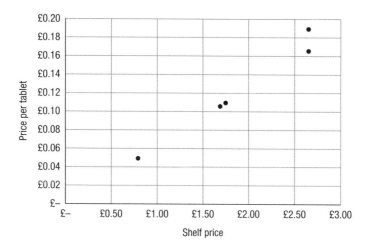

Figure 4.12 Paracetamol: Price per tablet for various price points shows vastly higher prices for the same functionality

You can see that the horizontal axis in Figure 4.12 is the price point, or price charged for the packaged product, whilst the vertical axis shows the price per 500mg tablet. Here, the same active 500mg of paracetamol is being sold at a price range of almost 400%.

SO, THE PRODUCT IS THE SAME, EXCEPT FOR PACKAGING AND BRAND

This fact, demonstrated above, perhaps shouldn't surprise us. We've been programmed from birth by advertising and company messaging to accept without question the value of brand, and its emotional value.

These examples highlight the role and importance of the way the product (or service) is portrayed and branded. Ultimately, this is about differentiation and understanding what creates value for the customer.

This begs the obvious question: What can you do to improve your packaging and brand, adding value for customers at the same time? If we think about the charts where products sell at higher prices, we can think of this as a 'value ladder' – so what can you do to move your perceived value up the 'value ladder', to qualify yourself for the more profitable customers? However, we'll come on to more ideas of how to bring about these kind of positive changes later in the book.

These kinds of questions and analyses encourage healthy customer-centric thinking, because to answer the questions you need to put yourself in the customer's shoes. Always a worthy exercise, this helps develop customer empathy and offers insights into how to make customers' lives better, and if you are reading this book, then hopefully charge them correctly for doing so.

In his seminal book *Thinking, Fast and Slow,* Daniel Kahneman, the father of behavioural economics, explains much of the machinery in our brains that drives decision making, and hence how decisions are made. We shall touch upon this work later in the book.

So far, we've seen how essentially the same products can occupy different price points in a category, now let's consider some more strategic elements of pricing.

EXERCISE

Produce your own pricing scattergram

It can be a useful exercise to produce a scattergram for your own products or services. It's useful because it gives you a top-level view of how your products are positioned in terms of performance and price.

The exercise causes you to think about relative merits of competing (or complementary) products and the trade-offs between them. It's also often fascinating to work with customers to understand their perception of the positioning map – sometimes your perceived performance is very different to that of customers'.

To do the exercise:

1. *Make a list of all your competitors and gather intelligence on their price points.*

2. *Consider the question of perceived performance and relative merits between the competing products.*

3. *Next, populate one or both of the following two charts (you can populate the second one if the products or service is sold in differing unit quantities).*

   a. **Price vs perceived performance**

   Plot the position of each of your products and those of the competitors' offerings. The vertical axis will show the various price points being occupied in the market. Since the horizontal axis will show the relative performance levels, those offerings which occupy the further right-hand side positions offer more value for money.

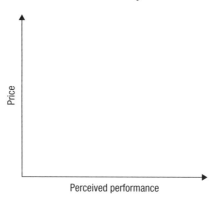

   b. **Price per unit vs perceived performance**

   If your product or offering is sold at different unit volumes (this can include service offerings through metrics such as hourly rates), then you can also populate the following chart. Again, the further to the right an offering is, the more value for money it offers.

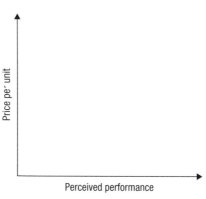

4. *Now ask about the relative price points. What do they say about the offerings? Are they consistent with a market that ranks quality efficiently? Are there any surprises or anomalies?*

5. *If there are multiprice-point offerings for a given company, for example if there are multiple versions of the same product, think about the relative positions between them. Are they clusters around certain price points? Does this suggest opportunities to occupy different price points in order to move either vertically up or down, and/or horizontally left or right – and how could these be perceived by the market?*

6. *Are there positions occupied by your products that seem illogical? Are there new and better positions that you can move them to?*

7. *Finally, revisit the question of perceived value: What factors are these measures of perceived value based upon? Are there ways to influence or change these in a way that is beneficial to your business?*

Guidance: This is a powerful exercise that can be used in various ways, as suggested above. A common question is how the data can be gathered: competitor price point information may be already known or can be gained by research – desk research, such as web searches for price lists, or via mystery shopping – (a bona fide technique, entailing paying a researcher to simulate being a prospective customer and engaging in a purchase process with competitors to gather various forms of intelligence). Calculating perceived performance can be done by comparing features and benefits, although, once again, some research can be very valuable to uncover what customer-relative perceptions are for the various offerings.

COMPANIES PLAY GAMES

We saw earlier on that companies sell exactly the same product at multiple price points.

They also sell the same product for different purposes at different price points. For example, companies selling soap found that when selling a face soap rather than a hand soap, they could charge a higher price, despite the actual soap being identical.

There was a legal case where painkiller brand Nurofen was sued and then fined A\$6 million by a court in Australia for selling an identical product for different uses at double the price. The Australian federal court ruled that the brand's Nurofen Back Pain, Nurofen Period Pain, Nurofen Migraine Pain and Nurofen Tension Headache products made false claims in that they had the same active ingredient despite costing about double the price of standard Nurofen.[5]

In general, people will pay more for a product that has a specific purpose than for one which is more generic. The idea that the product is specialised suggests it is worth more and therefore should cost more. Looking at cold and flu products on the pharmacy shelf, many of them have additional performance statements on them, such as good to aid sleep, or good for allergies – however, a look at the ingredients tells us that they are often actually identical, apart from some food colouring and the information on the packaging.

For example, Nytol is a sleep aid medication and its active ingredient is diphenhydramine hydrochloride.[6] By contrast, Histergan is a medication for hay fever and allergies – however, its active ingredient is the same diphenhydramine hydrochloride.[7] There's also antihistamine cream, which is a soothing treatment for reactions that skin can sometimes experience due to allergies or insect stings – guess what, it's diphenhydramine hydrochloride.[8] In all these case, the medication may work exactly as described; however, they are being packaged and positioned for specific purposes.

HOW ABOUT WHEN PRODUCTS ARE REALLY BETTER – CAN YOU BE THE CHEAPEST AND THE BEST?

It's always interesting to ask entrepreneurs what their product advantages are. It's equally interesting to ask them about their pricing strategy. It's surprising how often they will explain that they have a new product offering far superior features and performance than any competition, and yet it will sell for a price point 30% cheaper than competitors.

This double aim of being both better and cheaper is rarely sustainable. It can sometimes be possible if there is a fundamental and structural reason that the new offering can genuinely be cheaper than anyone else. For example, if a company has developed a new technology that allows it to produce a superior product at a fraction of the manufacturing cost of existing competitors, and this advantage is permanent in that it has an infallible trade secret as to how it works, or bullet proof intellectual property protection to stop others copying it. If this is not the case (i.e. almost always), then their technical advantages will either eventually be copied or ignored by the market.

After all, if the new product genuinely has great advantages over competitors, and these advantages are going to be genuinely valued by customers, then why not charge a higher price than the competitors?

YOU CAN BE THE CHEAPEST, OR YOU CAN BE THE BEST, BUT YOU CAN'T BE THE CHEAPEST AND THE BEST

As stated above, usually, this claim of superiority and low price by these high-growth businesses is not financially viable, and this is due to at least two underlying problems.

1. CONFUSING COMPETITORS' COSTS WITH THEIR PRICES

Where the business has done some analysis, usually the pricing claim is benchmarked against the current market price, i.e. the competitor's selling price. However, this does not at all consider what the costs are for that competitor. For example, if a competitor is selling at $100, it could be that their gross margin is 80% and their variable costs are actually only $20. This means that going in at a 30% saving, e.g. at $70, just means that the existing competitors can match the $70 comfortably, or worse, reduce their price to $20 (their break-even at the margin) until the new competitor goes bust, after which they can go back to normal.

This is a form of competitive response whereby the existing players in a market counteract a new threat that enters their space. This competitive response is quite powerful since the established market leaders have the highest market share, which means they are often the highest volume sellers, and volumes convey much higher economies of scale, which conveys a cost advantage. So, they are always going to win a price/cost war. It's possible that a large competitor may ignore a small company that is undercutting it, but that's not a solid strategy for growth.

2. IGNORING THE NEED FOR A HEALTHY MARGIN TO POWER FUTURE GROWTH

In the scenario above, even if the company is able to sell at £70 without a strong competitive response, it's unlikely that they will have healthy profit margins. Early stage and smaller businesses usually don't have economies of scale, so their unit costs are higher than established companies. If they can't make a good margin then they will be permanently cash starved and unable to reinvest in R&D, staff training and recruitment, and all those other things that smaller high-growth companies need to flourish. Raising investment from banks or equity investors can temporarily delay any reckoning, but it would remain a long-term problem unless margins are increased.

MICHAEL PORTER'S COMPETITIVE ADVANTAGE

Michael Porter's famous work[9] demonstrates how an organisation can outperform its competitors through achieving sustainable competitive advantage. It identifies several strategies including cost leadership, differentiation leadership, as well as industry-wide or focused segment approaches.

We can demonstrate this simply (see Figure 4.13).[10] Looking at Figure 4.13, we can see the relationship between selling price and the likelihood of making a profit. We can see that in order to succeed (and to be profitable, to pay staff adequately and also reinvest in future product improvements for the customer) the strategy has to be either as a low-cost offering or a higher price offering. In between the two can be called being 'stuck in the middle', where it's difficult to make a profit, and being there is likely to lead to bankruptcy. This is where many nascent companies unwittingly place themselves.

The two broad strategies are explained in further detail below.

1. COST LEADER

Cost leader (or low-cost leader) strategies are those where everything about the design of the company and its offering is focused on minimising costs and maximising economies of scale.

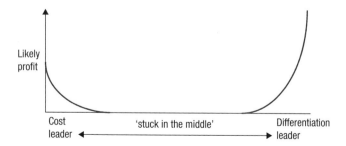

Figure 4.13 Michael Porter's Competitive Advantage: the two broad strategies can be successful but 'stuck in the middle' is problematic

It could be enabled by having a sustainable production cost advantage over competitors due to a unique piece of knowledge or technology often protected by some kind of legal framework, such as a patent.

More often it's enabled by an absolute dedication to be the most efficient and lowest cost at all things. This could mean paying suppliers the least amount of money possible, spending the least amount of money on rents, rates, on staff and on other costs. It's difficult to survive a long time, let alone flourish, with this type of low-cost strategy unless the company becomes systematically good at it. To work long term, it requires an almost religious fervour for keeping costs down. An example of this approach are the discount food and clothing retailers that have become popular in recent years – these focus on highly cost-efficient logistical supply chains and cost-effective retail environments. Other examples are discount airlines and discount traders who sell on third-party platforms such as eBay.

An example of the cost minimisation zeal that is sometimes at the heart a successful cost-leader's culture is IKEA. A manager at IKEA recounted the following story: When the group head of IKEA's sister finance group arranged to fly to the UK and visit a regional office in Nottingham, the staff offered to arrange a taxi to pick him up from the airport. Such a senior figure's time is, of course, very valuable. However, he insisted on taking a bus from the airport rather than spend the money on a taxi. This act of money saving by a very senior figure offers us at least two lessons: First, cost saving of this kind done well is a passion that can pervade all behaviours. Second, using opportunities for communicating and reminding staff of this philosophy and passion are important and not to be missed.

2. DIFFERENTIATION LEADER

By contrast, differentiation leader strategies are where the offering has been designed to be both valuable to the customer and to be different, and hopefully better in some way, from the offerings of competitors. Here the offering will not be low priced but instead will be at a premium price. This is 'a nice place to be' in that margins are healthy, and companies compete with each other on the value that they are creating for customers, not on their price.

STUCK IN THE MIDDLE

The vertical axis of the graph in Figure 4.13 is interesting. It indicates likely profit. Likely profit means that it's a useful combination of profit and also risk, or the likelihood of being able to achieve that profit. We can see that as a cost leader you can make money and as a differentiation leader you can also make money. However, the maximum profits are lower for cost leaders than those available to effective differentiation leaders. In other words, differentiation leaders have more potential to make higher profits. A good example of this differentiation leadership, higher prices and higher capability for profits is Apple's cash pile, or cash surplus, of $250 billion[11] – testament to a differentiation leader strategy done well.

However, those companies in between, as mentioned already, are 'stuck in the middle'. They are not adding enough value to customers' lives to be a differentiation leader and they are not cheap enough to be a cost leader. They are therefore attempting to be both low priced (which requires lower operating costs) and have better offerings (which requires higher operating costs). The chances of doing this successfully are low and the likelihood of company failure is higher. Being 'stuck in the middle' is often, therefore, a recipe for disaster.

Not adding enough value to customers' lives means the customer value proposition is not compelling enough. Essentially, what they are offering is not recognised as being suitably valuable by customers. Reasons for this might include inadequate (re)investment into processes that lead to effective product development, to the understanding of customer needs and to the effective communication of this proposition to customers.

Let's now briefly touch upon some different approaches to setting price (we'll visit this in more detail in Chapter 6).

SOME PRACTICAL PRICING METHODS

One of the most common questions I'm asked is 'How to set price?' Price setting can be a formidable task, not least because of the emotional aspects of dealing with uncertainty (often due to a lack of reliable and accurate data) and the strong desire to successfully gain new sales in order to grow. There are many philosophies or approaches to setting prices. A few are outlined here, starting with the three most popular, and we'll come back to this topic in more detail in Chapter 5.

COST-PLUS PRICING

Cost plus is one of the oldest and most widely understood methods for setting price. Here, the cost to produce (or supply, in the case of retail) the product is calculated and then a markup is applied. This approach has its origins in the industrial revolution. The industrial revolution was primarily a revolution of production technologies with mechanisation applied to manufacturing products. Perhaps that's why this approach has remained popular with producers and manufacturers.

Manufacturing processes are often complex to manage, successful operations management is highly detail dependent and managing large work forces in a manufacturing setting can be an ongoing challenge. Often these environments are rife with so called 'fire fighting', whereby a continual stream of time-critical problems and issues need to be resolved, taking away time from senior management. With all of this complexity, it's therefore easy for manufacturers to become introspective and focused on costs, rather than look outwards towards customers. Finding the bandwidth, or resource, to consider the market mechanism and look closely at changing customer needs is sometimes a challenge and can require a different mindset.

Just because it's convenient does not make cost-plus pricing the best pricing technique.

Practically, a cost-plus approach is also problematic because it assumes that costs can be accurately measured and don't change rapidly, plus it also ignores completely how much value is being created for the customer.

COMPETITOR OR GOING-RATE PRICING

With this method, prices are set to either match or have a relative position to competitors. This is easily visualised on a price-perceived performance scattergram similar to those earlier in this chapter, whereby the price point can be set with a reference to similar competitive offerings. Higher performance would imply a higher price, and lower performance a lower price, assuming this fact can be easily established.

VALUE-BASED PRICING

This is a more sophisticated technique, whereby the price is set by calculating how much value is created for the customer, and then the supplier takes a fair portion of that value as the price. Value-based pricing is particularly good for innovative products since there is no previously established price point. By extension of this, introducing innovative products to established markets offers an opportunity to, both, raise customer value and apply premium pricing.

OTHER PRICING APPROACHES

Skimming pricing

This approach uses a high price, usually for new innovative products at launch. Early adopter or cost-insensitive customers will buy at this higher price but volumes will usually be lower. Later, once the market is established, the strategy may change to penetration pricing to drive volume and increase market share.

Penetration pricing

Often applied after a period of skimming pricing, it uses a low price to rapidly gain market share or increase market penetration. This approach assumes that there is a price elasticity of demand, which is fine for very large and populous markets.

Perceived quality pricing

A higher price is used tactically to create an image of high quality and/or high performance. This approach is used for many premium brands and luxury products.

Periodic discounting

Usually this is related to a special event or a seasonal holiday where a temporary reduction in price is applied to entice customers to try a new product or purchase an additional one. However, overuse can effectively train customers to wait for discounts before purchasing.

Market discrimination pricing

The same product is sold at different prices in different markets, usually either reflecting different market rates with respect to competitors or different customer expectations in those markets. This is one reason why some products you see when travelling abroad are priced vastly higher or lower than you might otherwise expect to see in your home market.[12]

Negotiated or auction pricing

The seller and the customer bargain to set a price. An auction is an example of one seller and many buyers, where prices are bid upwards. A reverse auction is an example with many sellers and one buyer, where prices are bid downwards.

Loss leader pricing

A product is sold at a low and unprofitable price to entice customers to then buy other additional, more profitable, products. This is most famously used by supermarket advertising to get customers into the store where they are then subject to the wide temptations of the buying environment. The loss leader is usually placed at the back of the store. Customers enter to make one purchase and exit with an armful of products.

Bait pricing

This is the use of a low price for the most basic model in a range of products with the plan to upsell the customer to the more premium products in the range and therefore pay a higher price.

Pricing bundles

Several complementary products are bundled together and sold at one price. Sometimes the product is not available individually. Or, two products together offer a discount on the individual prices added together, but the customer increases their overall spend. When a product is only ever sold in a bundle, another advantage is in making it harder for customers to make price comparisons to competitive offers.

'What it's worth' pricing

The customer is asked to decide what they will pay. This can sometimes work well, especially if there are honest, generous customers and an emotional element to the offering. Examples of this include charitable works.

Surge pricing

Prices go up when the demand is highest. Examples of this include railway ticket fares at peak travel times and plane tickets when flights are popular and become full.

REACTIONS TO TEMPORARY DISRUPTIONS

During the global COVID-19 pandemic that took place during 2020–2022 many government administrations around the world took steps to help businesses survive the considerable disruption caused by the virus. In the UK, a package of tax cuts included a temporary reduction in the Value Added Tax (VAT) (or national sales tax) that businesses had to pay. The way that VAT works is that all businesses with sales over £85,000 must add a 20% VAT charge to all their sales. For B2B businesses, their customers would usually be able to reclaim the VAT paid, but for B2C businesses the consumer pays the full price – the 20% VAT charge is included in the price they pay.

Because the pandemic particularly affected B2C businesses which had relied on face-to-face interactions (such as restaurants and coffee bars), the UK government applied a reduced VAT rate of 5% to the hospitality industry (this later increased to 12.5%, as a stepping stone back to 20%). So, instead of having to apply a rate of 20%, a new tax rate of 5% was payable. There were two ways this could be implemented: companies could reduce their prices by 15%, passing on the saving to customers and, if the elasticity of demand holds true, thereby attract more sales, or they could hold their prices steady and increase their margins by 15% – this would effectively raise their own net selling price by 15%.

What did companies do? Did they reduce their prices to attempt to gain more business or accept the 15% effective price increase?

The overwhelming evidence is that most businesses retained their pricing and took the extra 15% margin for themselves. In a sense, they had passed-up on the opportunity to implement a 15% price cut that would not have had any cost to themselves, since VAT is calculated on top of their underlying price. Given there was no cost to them, the new 'base case' was a price that was 15% lower, which they then chose to immediately increase by 15%, back to the original price.

This interesting choice must be in some way associated with the framing of value and the asymmetric way that positives and negatives to a reference point are considered. It's possible it was influenced by the knowledge that the cut in VAT would only ever be temporary. However, sometimes people frame a loss from a reference point as being more painful and larger than a gain of the same magnitude. This cognitive bias is called *loss aversion* and may also go some way to explain this particular choice by businesses.[13]

WHAT CAN WE CONCLUDE ABOUT TRADITIONAL PRICING?

It's likely that using traditional pricing approaches won't give the insights required by high-growth companies to succeed. The gut feel, or basic understanding, we have regarding pricing is based on our experiences as consumers – where we are probably not aware of how our decision making and judgement have been manipulated by companies, or it's based on management theories devised in the 1930s for large corporations in slow-moving markets.

We've seen instead that products with identical functionality sell for a range of quite different prices, and in some cases at over 500% higher prices.

We've also seen that you usually can't be the cheapest *and* the best, and that attempting to be so is a recipe for failure. Therefore, for a growth entrepreneur to succeed, a new approach to pricing is required: smart pricing. We'll start to develop this theme over the next few chapters.

CHAPTER SUMMARY

■ Traditional pricing theory assumes price elasticity, efficient markets and rational well-informed players.

■ Yet, everyday, equivalent products are sold across price points different by upto 500%.

  ■ Most markets are therefore clearly imperfect.

■ This is particularly true in multiprice-point scenarios where various techniques are employed.

■ Generally, you can be the cheapest, or you can be the best, but you can't be the cheapest and the best.

■ Traditional pricing and market theory therefore doesn't lend itself to entrepreneurial success.

Things to consider

Product life cycle
Where in the product life cycle are your products, and what does this suggest in terms of price and competitive pressures?

Pricing scattergram
Where do your products sit in the landscape of competitive offerings? Can you see opportunities with unfulfilled niches?

Price or differentiation leader?
Which one are you? Or, are you stuck in the middle? (If so, how can you correct this?)

Pricing methods
Do you use cost plus, competitor-based or value-based pricing? Is this the most effective method, and if so, why/why not?

Chapter exercise

Produce your own pricing scattergram

CHAPTER 5

WHY IS PRICE SO IMPORTANT FOR GROWTH?

WHAT IS GROWTH?

If you are reading this book, then you are probably interested in 'growing' a business, whether it is small or large. So, let's spend a few minutes exploring the question: What is 'growth' and how is it achieved?

To grow a business, you usually need to increase revenue. Usually, an increase in revenue will also lead to an increase in profits. You can also grow profits by reducing costs, but there's a limit to how much cost can be removed before things stop working, so much more growth is available through increasing revenue.

Let's think about an example: Jane getting ready to sell lemonade at her lemonade stand.

Jane's revenue can be calculated by multiplying the value of each sales transaction by the number of transactions. In order to increase her sales, Jane can increase the price paid per lemonade, increase the number of lemonades sold in a typical customer transaction, increase the number of customers visiting the lemonade stand or increase how often any given customer buys from her.

Expressing this a little more formally, revenue can be easily expressed as

Revenue = (A) Value of each transaction

× (B) Number of transactions

Where (A), the value of each transaction, can in turn be broken down to

(A) Value of each transaction = (i) Price × (ii) Number of units

And (B), the number of transactions, can be further broken down to

(B) Number of transactions = (iii) Number of customers

× (iv) Number of transactions per customer

So, to increase revenues for a typical company:

- For (i), the price paid per unit in a transaction, a way needs to be found to increase the average unit price. Jane, for example, could increase the price from $0.50 to a higher price point, such as $0.75.

- For (ii), the number of units sold in a transaction, there needs to be an increase in units sold, either by on-sell, giving options to customers to put additional units in their transaction 'basket', and/or an upsell, to increase the size of the unit being bought. For Jane, she could offer a super-sized larger cup option at $1 or offer additional complementary products such as cookies for another $0.25.

- For (iii), the number of customers interacting with the company, there can be activities to increase the number of customers. (N.B. This is the usual focus of business development effort) Jane could try some advertising boards in the local area or get some coverage on the local radio station.

- For (iv), the number of transactions per customer, increase the frequency with which each customer purchases. Jane could offer a loyalty reward scheme to incentivise repeat visits or ask customers when they are likely to next be in the area.

So, in essence, to grow, a company must:

Increase the value per transaction (A) by

1. Increasing the price paid per unit

    and/or

2. Increasing the number of units sold per transaction

    and/or

Increase the number of transactions (B) by

1. Increasing the number of customers buying from them

and/or

2. Increasing the number of transactions per customer

We'll explore some ideas in Chapter 9 on how to achieve the above through the various factors. But for now, we're going to understand more about #1, the all-important price.

We've explored some of the background to pricing and to success, explored ideas about why profits are key to reinvestment and how important price is. So, let's ask the crucial question: Why is price so important for growth?

WHY IS PRICE SO IMPORTANT?

To begin to answer this, let's look at a simple example.

HOW MUCH MONEY DOES EACH COMPANY MAKE?

Imagine two companies, Company A and Company B. Company A has a lower unit price than Company B. It's £100 rather than Company B's £130. Perhaps as a consequence of this lower price, Company A has a higher conversion rate of sales from leads, where 60% of leads convert to sales, rather than 40% for Company B.

Here's a summary of that:

Company A	Company B
Price £100	Price £130
60% of sales convert	40% of sales convert
Profit ?	Profit ?

So, which company makes more profit and roughly how much more?

Yes, it's an unfair question. It depends on cost structure and gross margins and many other assumptions that could be made. Nonetheless try to divine an answer based on averages and reasonable assumptions for all variables.

The answer is surprising to many people:

Company A	Company B
Price £100	Price £130
60% of sales convert	40% of sales convert
Profit £400	Profit £800

Company A has profits of £400. Company B has profits of £800. Despite the lower conversion rate, Company B is not just more profitable but makes twice as much money as Company A.

(For those of you who wish to look, you can see the simple P&L statement in Appendix A.)

Why is this important? It's important because the #1 *resource for a company to grow is cash.* And we are going to use profit as an easy proxy (or approximation) for cash. Therefore, the more profit you can make, the more cash you will generate; cash you can reinvest back into the company.

Normally we think about growth as either increasing the number of customers, increasing the number of transactions per customer or increasing the average number of units per transaction. However, there is a largely overlooked source of growth: the opportunity to increase *price*. Higher prices increase revenues, but they can also transform the ability of the company to generate profits and cash which can then be reinvested.

DON'T TAKE MY WORD FOR IT

We looked at the very simple example of Company A and Company B to highlight the effect of price on profits (and through that, the effect on cash). However simplistic that example was, there's no need to take my word for it as plenty of research backs up the finding.

Here's some research from the venerable *Harvard Business Review* (*HBR*) that illustrates the same conclusion. A *HBR* report looked at 2,400 companies across many different sectors and asked the following question:

If you make a 1% improvement to price, or variable cost, or volume, or fixed cost, what is the average effect this would have on profit?

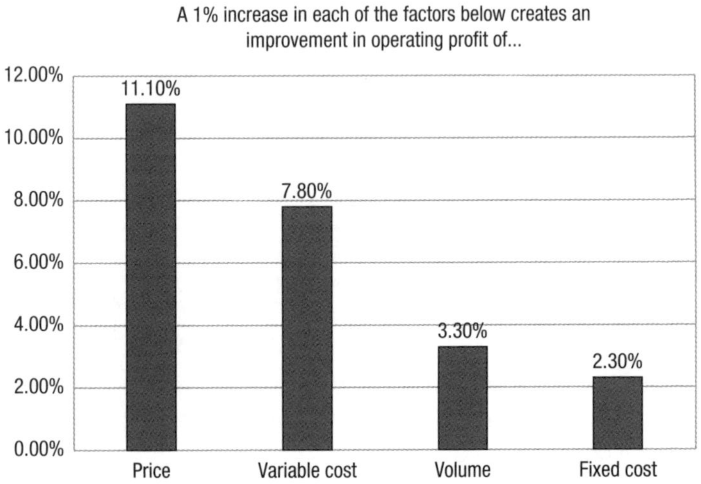

A 1% increase in each of the factors below creates an improvement in operating profit of...

Figure 5.1 Pricing is the biggest 'lever' to generate profit

The *Harvard Business Review* research[1] shows that price is, by far, the biggest 'lever' to increasing profits (see Figure 5.1).

It demonstrates that on average, across these 2,400 companies, increasing price by 1% gives an impressive 11.1% increase in operating profit. By comparison, decreasing variable cost by 1% gives a 7.8% improvement in operating profit – variable costs are those directly associated with the provision of the product or service, such as direct labour used in the supply or materials used in manufacturing. Increasing volume, or revenues, by 1% only gives a 3.3% improvement in operating profit. Reducing fixed costs is still less valuable, giving an improvement of just 2.3% – examples of fixed costs include overheads and central office costs.

There are two fascinating lessons from this *HBR* research: first, price is by far and away the biggest influence on profit. As we've said, it's the biggest 'lever' to increase profits. Profits in turn lead to cash generation. A business needs cash to grow, to supply the needs of working capital and for reinvesting in the company's operations, but also to secure the fantastic rates of return we'll come to see in Chapter 7. So, any growth plans should have price at their heart.

Second, when asking people what they think most about when growing a business, they normally say 'increasing sales'. In Figure 5.1, sales is labelled as 'volume' and only gives a 3.3% improvement on average. So, a percentage increase in sales contributes less than a third as much as the same increase in price. In other words, increasing price gives almost four times the 'bang per buck' compared to increasing sales.

This research is a great example to highlight how pricing is underappreciated. People who wish to grow their business usually think about growing sales, the top line. What perhaps they are missing is the important role that price has in growth. After all, would you rather grow your sales or grow your profits? Would you rather have double your current sales with the same profit or double the current profits irrespective of what increase in sales is required to achieve this?

The *Harvard Business Review* research shows an average taken across 2400 companies, so it's worth thinking about the structure of a specific company's financials – it could be that the price lever is actually even greater than the average figures shown above.[2]

Similarly, McKinsey published some research that highlights the effect price can have on businesses involved in distribution.[3] McKinsey looked at 130 global and publicly traded distributors and estimated that a 1% price increase would yield an astonishing 22% increase in EBITDA margins (Earning Before Interest, Tax, Depreciation and Amortisation – sometimes used as a proxy for cashflow), and a 25% uplift in stock price.

By contrast, McKinsey states:

'. . . an average distributor in 2018 would have to grow volume by 5.9 percent while holding operating expenses flat to achieve the same impact as a 1 percent price increase—no small feat, especially in mature markets where competition is fierce and growth often comes at the expense of profitability. That same distributor would have to reduce fixed costs by 7.5 percent . . . (assuming similar P&L structure) to deliver an equivalent uplift in EBITDA.

Our survey of more than 200 distribution customers across sectors indicates that pricing ranks sixth overall in what customers look for in a distributor. Price is the most important factor in winning deals on the key value items that represent the top 20 percent of products, which represent roughly 80 percent of an individual customer's purchases. But most customers are far less price sensitive on the many other items in their shopping baskets. This is where distributors have the biggest opportunities to raise margins . . .'

The McKinsey work shows that price has huge potential to transform the profitability and share price of distributors. It also shows that price is only the sixth-most important selection criteria for customers in that sector, with many other factors being more important (see Figure 5.2).

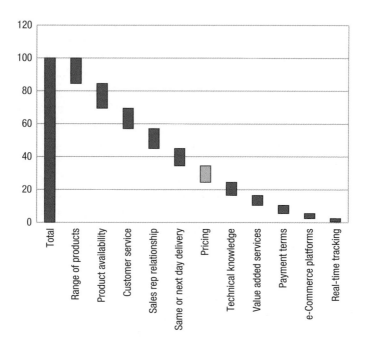

Figure 5.2 What customers rank most highly for B2B distributors

The analysis also offers some hints on how to make changes to increase profits – where customers are far less price sensitive for 80% of the products, which represent 20% of the value.

As well as highlighting the importance of pricing to increasing EBITDA, the research takes a sophisticated view of the whole product range and identifies that not all products are reviewed by customers with the same critical eye. Companies that can make this distinction tend to give themselves new opportunities.

THE TRUE COST OF DISCOUNTS

The *HBR* research above showed that, on average across 2400 companies, a 1% improvement to price gives a 11.1% improvement in operating profit.

What about in the other direction? What happens when salesforces give pricing discounts to customers, perhaps as incentives to 'get the sale'? What does this do to profits and what increase in sales is then required to recover the effects of the discount?

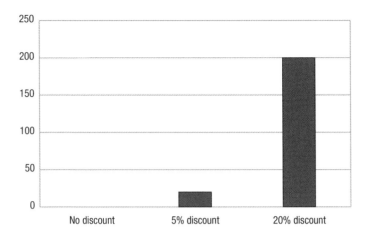

Figure 5.3 Additional sales required to regain profit lost by discounting

We can recreate a P&L (or income statement) with the same dynamics as the *HBR* average of the 2400 companies and then run two scenarios: a 5% and then a 20% pricing discount. The results are shown in Figure 5.3 (and a full version is in Appendix B). What is the effect on profits and what percentage of sales increase is required to offset the lower price? The answer is not at all obvious.

For the 'averaged P&L', a 5% price discount produces a 4% reduction in gross profit and an astounding 56% reduction in operating profit. To return the operating profit to the original level, what increase in sales is required? Is it 5%? Or 10%? In fact, a 20% increase in sales volume is required. Far higher than 5%. In other words, even if a 5% discount brings in more business, it will need to bring in 20% more business before 'breaking even'.

For a 20% discount it's much worse. The discount produces a 17% reduction in gross profit and a staggering 222% reduction in operating profit. The operating profit actually becomes strongly negative. To return the profits to the previous levels, sales will need to triple (a 200% increase). This means that the 20% discounted price will have to bring in three times more sales just to 'break even'.

It's interesting to ask ourselves whether CEOs and sales directors are fully aware of the drastic effect that even modest-sounding price discounts can have on the ongoing viability and reinvestment capability of their company.

	Base case	5% discount	To recover the discount		20% discount	To recover the discount	
Sales	100	95	_120%_	114	80	_300%_	240
Variable cost	**70**	70	_120%_	84	70	_300%_	210
Gross profit	30	25		30	10		30
GM%	_30%_	_26%_		_26%_	_13%_		_13%_
Fixed cost	**21**	21		21	21		21
Op profit	9	4		9	−11		9
% change to base case		_−55.6%_		_0.0%_	_−222.2%_		_0.0%_

EXERCISE

Working out your price leverage

It's a very straightforward exercise to work out how big a lever price is to any company. This is an exercise you can do for your own business.

To begin the exercise, start with a recent income statement (or profit & loss account, or P&L). The income statement will have revenues followed by a deduction of cost of sales (or cost of goods sold) which leads to a gross profit. From gross profit there will be a further deduction of operating expenses (or selling, general and administrative expenses), which leads to an operating profit. This is shown below.

	Example
Revenues (or sales)	_100_
minus cost of sales (or cost of goods sold)	_30_
= gross profit	_70_
minus operating expenses (or selling, general and admin expenses)	_40_
= operating profit	_30_

To do the exercise, calculate what a 1% change in price would produce. To do this, simply take the revenue figure and multiply it by 0.01. This is the increased revenue due to the price rise – let's call this number 'A'. Please see (A) below. Because there are no additional units being sold, there are no additional cost of sales, the number 'A' can therefore be added directly to the gross profit figure to give the new gross profit after the 1% price rise. Similarly, because there are no increases in operating expenses the number 'A' can be added to the existing operating profit to give the new operating profit (B).

	Original profit	New profit	
Revenues (or sales)	100	(A): 100˙0=1.01	
minus cost of sales (or cost of goods sold)	30		
= gross profit	70	70+1=71	
minus operating expenses (or selling, general and admin expenses)	60		
= operating profit	10	(B): 10+1=11	(C): 11/10= 10% increase

Comparing the new and original operating profit before tax will illustrate how much difference a 1% increase in price makes. If you divide the new operating profit figure (11) by the original figure (10), then subtract 1 and then multiply by 100 you will get the percentage increase in profit (C). In the example above it is 10%, which is to say that a 1% increase in price produces a 10% increase in operating profit.

The HBR research indicates that the average across 1,000s of businesses is about 11%, but your own figure may be much larger or smaller. This exercise highlights why it's sometimes said that 'any increases in price drop to the bottom line' – which is to say that since there are no increases in costs, any price increase goes directly to the profit line.

You can do this for your own company here.

	Original profit	New profit	
Revenues (or sales)		(A):	
minus cost of sales (or cost of goods sold)			
= gross profit		optional	
minus operating expenses (or selling, general and admin expenses)			
= operating profit		(B):	(C): % increase =

▶

Guidance: The exercise can be done using a current financial statement, or a historic or forecast statement. The key results will be in understanding what percentage profit increase is the result of a 1% change in price. You can either take the overall revenue figure (A) or you can take an individual product – if you have a fully costed P&L/income statement for the product. Both work, since price is proportional to revenues – as we saw in the formula at the start of this chapter. For an easier calculation, you can go from revenue (A) to operating profit (B), and ignore the gross profit change.

FUNDING REINVESTMENT

The ability to reinvest in a business is usually driven by the availability of cash, as we'll come to see in Chapter 7. The critical types of reinvestment are those which predicate and enable the future growth of the business. For example, improvements in customer experience, recruiting additional staff, training and equipping those staff with the necessary skills to move the business forward, investments in technology and new product development and, finally, acquiring new business through advertising and sales. Reinvestment is therefore critical to empower a business, to develop the capabilities required to pursue and deliver growth.

WHAT IS WORKING CAPITAL AND WHY DOES IT MATTER?

Perhaps you have heard the cautionary tale that the fastest way to bankrupt a business is to double or triple its sales rapidly? The phenomenon is certainly real and businesses do unfortunately 'go bust' each year due to growth. The reason this happens is usually working capital requirements.

Working capital is the lifeblood of any business. It's hugely important. It's the money that's tied up in the fabric of what the business does. Growing businesses must finance their growing needs for working capital.

Let's take a simple example to explain what this means: a factory manufacturing a product.

The usual business model for a manufacturing business is that it has a physical factory where the product is assembled or fabricated. Working capital for manufacturers is critical because it tends to define the time lag between when a company invests in manufacturing a product and when the company is paid for that product by a customer.

In the case of this example manufacturer, the factory may invest in raw materials, it may invest in machinery, it may invest in employees and it may utilise all of those resources to make a stockpile of finished products, which is then stored in a warehouse, which also has a cost associated with it. Only then is the finished product available for sale and, after a successful sale and delivery to a customer, there may be a delay in actually getting paid. In the case of B2B markets, where the customer is another business, often the manufacturer will have to wait 30, 60, 90 or even, in some dire cases, 180 days to get paid for that sale.

In this case, the time lag between the company having paid out cash in all the various steps to make a product available and then actually receiving payment from a customer in cash for that product can be very long. This is an example of the working capital cycle where companies are essentially investing cash into stock, which is stored for a while, then supplied to customers and then waiting a period of time to be paid for all that investment via the credit terms that the factory gives its customers.

Investment in this stock traps cash that's not released until a customer pays for something. If the business doubles in size by doubling sales, the size of the stockpile will nominally double too, as will the amount of cash tied up in this working capital cycle.

Long payment cycles of 30, 90 or even 180 days from when something is sold to a customer to when the customer actually pays is essentially a free loan from the factory to its customers. The size of this loan is proportionate to the annual sales. Therefore, if this business doubles in size, then the loan to customers doubles in size too. So, if a business doubles in size, so does the amount of cash tied up in these various forms of working capital.

Therefore, a quick and easy way to make a company go out of business is by growing the sales more quickly than the business is able to raise capital, or cash, to fund its working capital requirements. The pattern is this: the cash in the bank goes to zero, the account then becomes overdrawn, then the company is unable to pay its bills and then it fails. It can be a highly profitable business, but if there's no money in the bank to pay the bills, the business fails.

Which is why, when businesses grow too fast or without financial control, they so often become bankrupt through a cash crisis, whilst seemingly appearing viable because they were profitable.

For an example at the opposite end of the working capital spectrum, we can think about a B2C business selling to consumers online and having a B2B supply chain. If a company is selling a product to consumers, it's usual that the consumer pays immediately, usually via a credit card, or similar.

This retailer therefore receives full payment in cash through the credit card payment mechanism very quickly, sometimes within minutes. In supplying that product, the retailer calls upon its supply chain. In some examples the retailer may not even hold the stock of that particular product, and instead asks the supplier to send the product out to the consumer directly. This supplier then must wait 30 or 60 days to be paid by the retailer. By contrast, the retailer has received immediate payment from the consumer.

In this case we see a positive working capital cycle, where the retailer is being paid immediately by its consumer in advance of the product dispatching and is also essentially receiving a 'free loan' from its suppliers in the supply chain. Were the retailer to double their sales, it would have the benefit of doubling the loan it receives from its suppliers and therefore essentially it has a cash positive model, where the more it increases its sales the more self-funding the business becomes.

A nice analogy for working capital is the 'oil' or 'lube' in a car engine. If you remove the oil from the combustion engine in your car and try to drive somewhere, the engine will seize up and the car will come to a halt. The oil is essential to the engine working. If you design an engine that is twice the size, then, naturally, it will require twice as much oil as the smaller engine.

HIGHER PRICE, HIGHER CASH GENERATION

The *HBR* and McKinsey research show that a superior price gives disproportionally higher profits. Since the profit margin will be bigger, the level of cash generation will be bigger. Having more cash generated, even after whatever delays exist in an individual company's working capital cycle, will allow for easier funding of the working capital – critical for any growing business. This important role of price in supporting working capital is often forgotten.

Higher prices are therefore one of the most powerful ways to fund reinvestment, which enables businesses to grow fast and effectively. This link between reinvestment and pricing is usually similarly overlooked.

PRICE IS OFTEN A MESSENGER

Would you rather live in a £250,000 house or a £500,000 house?

Would you rather drive a £10,000 car or a £50,000 car?

Would you rather fly in a plane with a pilot earning $100,000 a year or $25,000 a year? Would you rather be operated on by a surgeon earning $80,000 or $400,000?

Even without any other information, price conveys many messages around quality and effectiveness. Price is therefore a strong messenger of quality. Low prices tend to indicate poor quality. Products that are priced relatively low compared to their competitors tend to be viewed by customers as perhaps being of lower quality, having less attractive features, perhaps being riskier. Therefore, we need to be aware of what messages we are sending customers when we set prices, and how those messages are framed by the customers' all-important decision-making process.

HOW ABOUT MARKET TESTING OR ENTERING THE MARKET WITH A LOW PRICE?

If you start with a low price, it's often difficult to raise it later. It's almost always easier to reduce prices than raise them afterwards!

More seriously perhaps, if you are testing a market with a temporarily reduced price, but you intend to sell in that market at a higher price later, then you won't actually be doing a market test. It won't represent your actual plan. You'll be doing a test for a business case that you don't intend to follow, so it won't be a valid proof for the offering that you wish to actually bring to market. Companies that do this can end up with a false positive and enter the market but then find that they can't operate at the higher price that they should have tested in the first place.

It's therefore important when doing market testing to get the pricing right – a price point that is neither too high to be viable, nor too low to provide business success.

DIFFERENTIATING YOURSELF

The McKinsey research above highlighted that when customers buy, few of them select the very cheapest offering. Instead, most compare the features and benefits of the available offerings, the attributes they have, to find a value 'sweet spot' that they feel is best for them. So, given that there will be an acceptable price range for most products and services, there is an opportunity to differentiate your offering through the use of price.

EXAMPLE

In the UK, The Alchemist[4] is a company that supports much higher prices via a high-value offering and a differentiation strategy. The Alchemist's chain of cocktail bars sells not just premium spirits and cocktails, but also offers consumers a unique experience based on an almost theatrical delivery of unusual and entertaining drinks which often smoke, morph and change colour and shape.

By deepening their offering and understanding what groups of friends desire when they go out for an evening of entertainment, The Alchemist has developed a unique offering that can command a premium price. A comparison to similar chain cocktail bars in the same city suggests The Alchemist's average cocktail price is 12% above that of upscale competitors.

CHAPTER SUMMARY

■ Research by *HBR* shows that price is by far the biggest 'lever' for increasing profits.

   ■ Over three times more powerful than an equivalent sales increase

■ Pricing is therefore a powerful way to increase profits, helping support working capital needs.

■ Profits also lead to cash generation, which leads to reinvestment.

   ■ Reinvestment can grow overall company value at compound growth rates.

■ Premium prices with a well-differentiated valuable product should be a key aim, not underpricing through a lack of confidence.

■ It's important to remember that price is often seen as a messenger of quality and effectiveness.

Things to consider

Price leverage
Work out your price leverage *x*%
Is this higher or lower than your competitors?

Working capital
Do you have a positive or negative working capital cycle?
How does this affect your cash requirements for growth in the future?

Chapter exercise

Working out your price leverage

CHAPTER 6

PRICE SHOULD ALMOST NEVER BE 'COST PLUS'

THE END OF COST-PLUS PRICING

Such is this book's focus on understanding customer value and using that understanding to help set price that an alternative book title might have been *The End of Cost-Plus Pricing*. However, this chapter is here because, despite many people agreeing with the chapter title, there are still far too many businesses using the cost-plus technique to set their prices.

Let's remind ourselves of the cost-plus technique: put simply, it's an approach where the price is based on a calculated cost of production, and then a markup is applied to derive the price. For example, if a product costs £50 to produce (or to buy in from the supply chain) the company will price it at £100; based on cost plus a 100% mark up.

As mentioned earlier, cost plus has its roots in the industrial revolution when products were being manufactured by industrial processes for the very first time with greatly increased usage of mechanisation – high volume processes which were suitable for recording and measurement. Hence, these exciting new production technologies made it natural to focus on production cost. However, what was a good idea in the market 200 years ago isn't necessarily good today.

Why 'almost never' in the chapter title rather than 'never'? There are some exceptions where cost plus is the correct, or only feasible, pricing strategy – for example, if a supplier has a contract that requires it to open its 'books' (its financial records) to a customer to allow for an agreed margin to be calculated and added in order to calculate the price. These types of contracts are relatively rare, but do still exist, and in these cases cost plus is designed in as a 'necessary evil'. Nonetheless, in general, cost plus is a price-setting approach best consigned to history.

MAKING THE VALUE PIE BIGGER: INTEGRATIVE VS DISTRIBUTIVE EXCHANGES

For those wishing to understand the context within which a commercial sale and purchase takes place and then use this understanding to help find a way to set a price, there are some valuable lessons from the theory of negotiations. In particular, there is a useful piece of negotiations theory that illustrates two pure forms of negotiation: distributive and integrative.

Distributive negotiations are also sometimes called 'win lose' or zero-sum negotiations. Imagine an apple pie which is to be split between two parties.

The size of the apple pie is fixed, and the principal task of the negotiation is to decide how the apple pie is sliced and shared between the participants. In the case of a two-party negotiation, it's possible that the apple pie will be split 50:50 or 75:25, or even 100:0. It's also of course possible that the negotiation will fail, and neither party will enjoy the pie. As an example, the pie can be thought of as the amount of value at stake in the negotiation. In other words, the size of the pie is equal to the amount of profit that the supplier could potentially make *plus* the amount of value the buyer would receive from the purchase. In B2B, this value for the purchaser is often the value of cost savings the use of the product will subsequently deliver and/or the net value of an increase in profitable sales (see Figure 6.1).

It's sometimes called a zero-sum negotiation because the size of the pie is fixed. The greater the slice one party gets (a positive gain, e.g. +1) then the other party's slice is reduced by the same amount (a negative loss, −1) – adding the two together equals zero, hence zero sum, or no change in the overall size of the pie despite the outcomes. The product produces a certain amount of value for the buyer and seller, so the size of the pie is fixed, and the negotiation is principally about splitting this value – often through setting the price. The higher the price one party pays, the less pie value they get, the more the other party gets.

Examples of distributive types of exchanges include most purchases of a product. A simple example is the purchase of a used car at a show room: although a price is shown on the car, there is always some bargaining potential. The used car dealer can make a certain profit, which is largely dictated by the price they achieve[1] in reselling the car. The buyer gains value from the purchase and use of the car, although this reduces

Figure 6.1 Distributive apple pie of value: one party's gain is another's loss

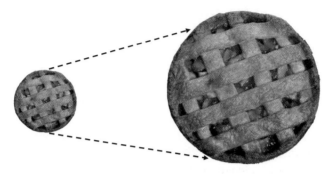

Figure 6.2 Integrative apple pie of value: finding ways to make it bigger benefits everyone

according to how much they pay for the car. If the price moves up or down via the bargaining process, one party gains, the other loses (see Figure 6.2).

By contrast, integrative negotiations are also called 'win win' or value building. In these kinds of negotiations, the size of the apple pie is not fixed. Instead of focusing on how to split up the pie, which is usually about setting the price in distributive exchanges, the focus is on making the pie bigger. If the pie can be made bigger, then the value generated is bigger, hence a 'win win', whereby both parties are better off even after the pie is finally divided. This process of making the pie bigger is of particular interest to entrepreneurially minded price setters because it poses the obvious question of 'how can the pie be made bigger for the customer?' If the pie can be made bigger, then there's more value available to all parties and this includes a potentially higher price.

Please keep in mind this idea of increasing the size of the pie. Making the pie bigger offers a real opportunity to make products more valuable – routes to do this could include the features and benefits of the product, the way the product is sold, the way the product is communicated, and more broadly and most importantly in consumer goods, the amount of emotional value that can be attached to the product (often via the messages that accompany the product). More about emotional value will be covered in Chapter 6, but let's now review some pricing methods in more detail.

THE MANY DIFFERENT PRICING METHODS

'. . . In most forms, prices are determined by intuition, opinions, rules of thumb, outright dogma, top management's higher wisdom, or internal power fights . . .'

Hermann Simon, Confessions of the Pricing Man

The quotation above from pricing pioneer extraordinaire Hermann Simon reflects the reality of how pricing is formulated in many organisations. Too often, pricing is either misunderstood, feared, ignored or subject to the politics of the organisation.

In all of these cases, what is missing is a formal recognition of the importance and influence of pricing and then the creation of a pricing process and methodology for the organisation to use to ensure it's maximising the potential that smart pricing offers. Let's look at some of the key pricing methods from Chapter 3 in more detail.

COST PLUS

This is one of the most traditional approaches with its process-oriented roots in the industrial revolution. If you can calculate your manufacturing cost as, for example, £100 then you can set the price at £100 plus a suitable margin, say a 60% uplift, therefore 'manufacturing *cost plus* 60%', producing a price of £160. The method is said to provide some comfort to its users because, assuming they know their costs correctly, they can feel assured that they will be selling at a profit.

The biggest problem with this approach is that it is entirely introspective. It's based on the perception of what is going on within the company processes. It pays no attention to how much the product is actually worth to customers, nor what competitors are doing – both of which can be really important reference points to understand the broader business context. From a company culture perspective, companies that are customer-centric, that are aware and in touch with what customers are feeling and thinking tend to be better placed for business success. The introspection encouraged by cost plus tends to lead company culture away from this, to produce cultures that are more isolated and less customer aware.

Cost plus also assumes that the company is actually able to measure its costs accurately – something that is notoriously difficult. There are many complexities within cost accounting, all kinds of assumptions are required in calculating costs, such as assumptions about volumes and overhead allocation, and how these costs change over time. These assumptions are usually based on historical figures[2] so the future may well prove to be different, in which case the costs won't work out correctly. To some extent this explains why some companies thinking they are making a profit actually sometimes end up with a loss – current costs are difficult to accurately judge.

Cost of production should, usually, be therefore largely irrelevant in pricing decisions, other than as a 'sanity check' via the accounting function to confirm that healthy margins are in fact being made.

Use of cost plus is especially common for manufacturers (whose businesses require them to have plenty of cost data), but for any given company, just because so much time and effort is spent measuring different forms of cost for control purposes, does not mean cost should be central in pricing decisions. As one 'known' parameter amongst many 'unknowns' for any commercial endeavour, its usefulness tends to be overplayed.

EXAMPLE

Cost-plus pricing in furniture manufacturing

A high-end furniture company in the UK designs and makes unique furniture to order based on customer requirements and their own artisanal origination. With a discerning clientele, they have been successful to date, but they are not meeting their growth ambitions.

A key aspect of their business decision making is, how should they be setting their price when each piece is unique? Most businesses in this position revert to cost-plus pricing, because there's a lack of external comparators, and because of the need to feel confident they are making a profit.

It would seem highly likely that they are underpricing. However, how should they set price in order to realise the value of their business?

Perhaps the best answer is that the price should be set by what customers are willing to pay for something that is unique – particularly because there are no external reference points that can be used to say what the price should be. This problem of a lack of reference points would presumably be as strong for the customer as it is for the manufacturer.

Conducting useful market research, perhaps by setting market experiments, would help them to establish what budgetary appetite their customers actually have, and, even better, what opportunities there may be for increased value recognition by their customers – such as enhanced emotional value and an improved customer experience.

However, they actually set price by cost plus, with all of its limitations and problems. Worse than this, they take their anticipated cost, which as we know may well prove to be incorrect, and then apply a markup taken from another industry, which is not at all related to the dynamics of their particular industry. A different industry, or market, is likely to have very different levels of value derived by the customer and a different relationship to levels of production cost.

Cost plus was clearly not meeting their needs and a change in their pricing philosophy was required to unleash the true potential of the business.

COMPETITOR-BASED PRICING

Competitor-based pricing is quite a common approach and can be used either alone or in tandem with other pricing techniques. It essentially asks how much do competitors charge for a similar product in the category? Since a company may be trying to look at the customer perspective, it will think customers compare the options available to them and one of the key things they compare is price. Therefore, a company will base its price on the levels used by the competition. In other words, it pegs its pricing to the levels that competitors have chosen – however, it does this irrespective of whether those price points are based on compelling rationale by competitors or whether they are arbitrary.

Although competitor-based pricing is laudable as a very commercial approach, it does have some problems associated with it. One problem is a lack of regard for what value is being generated for parties in the transaction. Perhaps the value generated for customers is far higher than recognised in the current pricing structure? Yet another problem is that it assumes that the competitors and customers are rational players making rational decisions. Much of the recent research in behavioural economics, and how customers make decisions, suggest this is rarely the case.

Competitor-based pricing is also supported by the price scattergram diagrams we looked at in Chapter 4. When doing the scattergram exercise, one of the challenges is in assessing where along the performance axis the particular offering should be plotted. This problem is worse when offerings are not easy to compare. Similarly, a challenge of using competitor-based pricing is how to compare competing offerings if they are well differentiated.

Another common problem with start-ups and high-growth businesses is that entrepreneurs often think they can be successful by underpricing with respect to competitors. In other words, they think by being 'just a little' cheaper they will gain business more easily and be successful. Earlier in the book we examined why this can be very dangerous. In some industries, profit margins can be large (research suggests that this is usually for a relatively short period of time) and competitors are making great margins, so undercutting their prices can still drive growth – albeit this can be more due to luck than judgement. However, for most industries this won't be the case, and the arbitrary nature of undercutting competitors means making margins dangerously low. Even worse, longer term it could trigger a damaging price war. Escalating price competition in such a war means that few companies can survive, let alone thrive.

VALUE-BASED PRICING IN BUSINESS MARKETS

A better strategy in most circumstances is linking price to customer value. Value-based pricing links the price to the benefits enjoyed by the customer. It asks, 'What is the value to the client?' and then takes a portion of this by asking a fair price, the remainder of the value being the customer's.

Thinking about customer value also opens the door to a plethora of valuable approaches and a healthy analysis of what the customer's buying environment is actually like. In other words, how they make decisions.

A typical way of doing value pricing compares two scenarios to see what value the product creates. The first scenario is the base case, what happens if the customer does not use the product being offered. The second scenario introduces the product and asks what advantages are now being enjoyed by the customer. Ideally, in this scenario the advantages are quantified. This quantification is usually expressed in monetary or quantitative terms – how much better off is the customer by using the product? Usually, especially in B2B, this tends to be either a cost saving – how much money do they save by using the product – or an increase in profits via sales – how much extra profit do they gain by using the product.

This can be thought of as the apple pie of value – the value generated in integrative 'win win' negotiation transactions. Once you have a figure for how much value is being generated you can then split this value up between yourself and the customer. This split can vary by sector, but by way of example, in B2B services and software, typically between 15% and 25% of the value is retained by the supplier, whilst 75% to 85% goes the buyer. The 15% to 25% of value retained by the supplier is called the price. However, the actual level varies by industry based on the underlying economics of that industry, and a particular sector tends to have norms.

It's worth noting that this analysis is far easier to do when selling to a business (B2B) as opposed to selling to a consumer (B2C), because consumers tend to be less rational decision makers than businesses, and also because many of the advantages generated for consumers in sophisticated product categories tend to be intangible, such as emotional value, and are therefore harder to quantify. Nonetheless, value-based pricing is a worthy cause to pursue and the analysis it demands can produce interesting insights.

EXAMPLE

Pricing the $1m gadget

Let's imagine a company has created a new 'gadget' that creates $1,000,000 of value for customers. Perhaps the gadget is a unique and innovative device that produces a large percentage saving in fuel cost – and for an average customer this amounts to $1,000,000. So, if the company has created a new 'gadget' that creates $1,000,000 of value for customers, and let's say there are no competitors or substitutes, what's a fair price to ask for this gadget?

Many will say $500,000 – whereby, having created a new 'pool' or 'apple pie' of value of $1,000,000, it is shared equally with the customer 50:50. In this case, half of the apple pie is retained by the supplier as the price, whilst half is enjoyed by the customer by purchasing and using the device. Some would argue that a rational customer would accept a price as high as $999,999, in that they still make $1 of value, although this doesn't factor in the aggravation and time costs of making the purchase and learning to use the new gadget. In many cases, and it varies in different industries and markets, companies tend to actually claim 15% to 25% of this new value as the price. So, let's say $250,000 in this example.

Now, let's add some more information. If the cost accounting department reports that the gadget costs $900 to manufacture, what price should you now charge the customer? Again, let's assume there are no substitutes or competitors.

The answer is of course the same, $250,000. The fact that the cost of production is so low is irrelevant compared to the value created for the customer and the situation with respect to competitors and substitutes.

This is an overly simplified example and ignores the role of competitors and substitutes but, nonetheless, makes an important point. Many companies make the mistake of not understanding this relationship between value creation, price and costs and whether they should or should not be linked.

Value-based pricing is an integrative way to look at increasing value generation. Integrative value generation assumes that in the case of a sales transaction value is being generated. If the transaction did not take place, then both parties would be worse off. The act of investigating and building a sales case plus delivery of a better solution builds the value. This is as opposed to distributive or zero-sum transactions where there is no increase in value generation throughout the transaction process, just the competitive division of the value between parties.

A key aspect of value-based pricing is, therefore, to assess, and hopefully work to increase, the amount of value that is being generated for the customer, as this is a gateway to a bigger pie – more value and premium prices.

VALUE-BASED PRICING IN CONSUMER MARKETS

Value-based pricing can be equally powerful in consumer markets, although the challenges in using this approach can be different. Whilst in business markets it's probably easier to calculate the financial advantages of using one product over another, it's usually less clear in consumer markets. There are two reasons for this.

The first reason is that the typical consumer is not a calculating machine making highly considered purchasing decisions in the same way that a company might employ a professional purchasing agent. Instead, many consumer purchases are made either on impulse, or, more broadly, via the system thinking outlined by Daniel Kahneman in *Thinking, Fast and Slow*: there are two systems, System 1 thinking is high speed and intuitive, driven by instinct. This is in contrast to System 2 thinking, which is slower, conscious and more logical. Surprising many, Kahneman shows that instinctive System 1 does much of the decision making. This goes some way to explain why many consumers appear to be open to making irrational purchase decisions.

Furthermore, consumers do not, in general, exhaustively research options to maximise value as they have a limited capacity to process information. Instead, they will stop when they are *sufficiently satisfied.* Nobel Prize winner Herbert A. Simon termed the expression 'satisficing' as a mix of satisfy and suffice to capture the essence of the idea.[3]

The second reason is that many of today's most valuable consumer brands achieve superior prices and profits through large amounts of intangible value in their offerings. These intangible elements may include security, emotional value, and other associated 'soft elements' often associated with B2C brands. From the perspective of setting a price, it is therefore less straightforward to use quantitative measurements of these intangible elements. Instead, a more qualitative approach must be used.

Price is, of course, also a strong indicator of performance or quality. As we will see in the next chapter, the evidence tells us that consumers generally feel that the higher the price the higher the quality must be.

In any case, value-based pricing is hugely effective in consumer markets and, very much in line with the traditional 4 Ps of marketing, the setting of price is something best done in parallel to designing the overall product and value offering. In general, the higher emotional content and other intangible elements of the offering, the higher the price point.

EXAMPLE

Seedlip Drinks

Seedlip is an example of a UK company successfully avoiding cost-plus pricing. Seedlip produces non-alcoholic spirits by taking botanical ingredients and putting them through a six-week maceration, distillation, filtration and blending process.[4] In particular, it has found a role as a non-alcoholic replacement for gin in a variety of cocktails.

How should Seedlip position a non-alcoholic spirit when the competitors are traditional alcoholic drinks? In a traditional sense, Seedlip is a drink that contains less, not more.

In terms of selling price, a well-known brand of gin would typically cost £15 to £20 for a 70cl bottle. Premium brand gins sell at higher price points, typically £30 to £35 for a 70cl bottle, whilst budget gins range from £10 to £15.

Furthermore, in the UK, the tax excise duty on a 70cl bottle of alcoholic gin is £8.05,[5] and this is included in the gin retail selling price. Seedlip, in contrast, need not pay this tax, since the product contains no alcohol.

Where do you think Seedlip should position their price point?

In actual fact, Seedlip typically retails for £22 to £30 per 70cl bottle.

Seedlip's manufacturing costs are not in the public domain. However, they clearly have a saving of £8.05 in duty over other brands containing alcohol. Despite this saving, their price point is at least equivalent, and in many cases higher, to those of traditional gins.

This indicates a great confidence in their value proposition. Consumer reviews reflect the value that users find in the product and mention the benefits of having a cocktail drink option that avoids alcohol but is still socially acceptable and well flavoured. The premium nature of the product appears to give it further credibility as an alternative choice to traditional alcoholic gins.

Seedlip is a good example of a company using value-based pricing – setting price by value derived, not by cost plus.

TOOLS TO BUILD EMOTIONAL VALUE

BUILDING THE BRAND

The Chartered Institute of Marketing has a definition of brand as follows:[6]

> '. . . A brand is really a symbol of everything the business stands for, what it promises customers – and, increasingly, what it actually delivers . . .'

Branding is an exercise in creating real value over and above the purely functional elements of the offering, in a similar way to the different water products in Chapter 4 – the water molecule is identical, the only differences are in the packaging and in the branding, and yet the price difference is 600%.

In classical business theory, much of this difference can be attributed to the brand and in the emotional value elements that it delivers. For premium-priced products, there's an element of chicken and egg here – do customers really recognise the value in the brand before or after the very strong value messaging power of the indicated price? It's probably a philosophical debate, but for all price points there's no doubt that brand and price both working together can convey a substantial messaging payload and build perceived value.

There's an opportunity therefore to use this role of brand in expressing emotional value – the creation of value beyond tangible or utilitarian value.

BUILDING VALUE IN THE BRAND AND IN THE OFFERING

There are also some useful hints of how to build value for customers in a value pyramid hierarchy originally developed by Bain & Company and published in *Harvard Business Review*.[7]

Somewhat similar to Maslow's famous hierarchy of needs (Figure 6.3), this pyramid is based on research with 8,000 consumers and related to 50 different companies. It highlights the elements which can be 'accessed' to build perceived value, which is particularly useful in considering the design of the messaging and/or benefits associated with a product.

The pyramid is in four layers:

- **Functional layer** – these are the most basic elements of value delivery. They sit at the bottom of the pyramid but are nonetheless important and significant sources of value. They include saves time, simplifies, makes money, reduces risk, organises, integrates, connects, reduces effort, avoids hassles, reduces cost, quality, variety, sensory appeal and informs.

- **Emotional layer** – the next level up from Functional, these add elements of emotional value and are a usefully broad variety of potential sources of great value. These include reduces anxiety, rewards me, nostalgia,

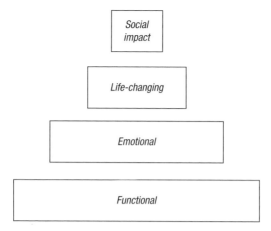

Figure 6.3 Brand value pyramid hierarchy

design/aesthetics, badge value, wellness, therapeutic value, fun/entertainment, attractiveness and provides access.

- **Life-changing layer** – although fewer in number as we go up the pyramid, these elements provide heightened value perception through a sense of achievement, or creating a sense of optimism, affiliation and so on. These elements include provides hope, self-actualisation, motivation, heirloom, affiliation and belonging.

- **Social impact layer** – the sole element on this level is self-transcendence. This level can change the world, and providing the consumer with a role in achieving this can add value. For example, every time a customer makes a purchase, a good action is triggered such as planting a tree, giving someone impoverished some help, or making a charitable donation.

If you'd like to explore each of the elements in much more detail, I've given a link in the footnote.[8]

Using the pyramid to assess Apple's iPhone offering, at the functional level the phone has a role as a calendar and 'to do' list – helping *organise* the user. It *connects* people together via various forms of communication. There are a *variety* of models, sizes and prices to suit different customers. They are well made and very high *quality.* The productivity aspects of the phone, such as accessing the internet, *save time* for the user. Having these facilities 'in the pocket' *reduces effort* too.

At the emotional level, it offers *fun and entertainment* through a highly accomplished web store of apps and games – Apple was the first to develop such a large app store. Often occupying the highest price points in its categories, it also has *badge value,* or even snob appeal, as a high prestige product. It's famous for both its physical *design* but also its graphical interface – both of these help customers to find it rewarding to own and use.

At the life-changing level, customers feel part of an Apple community and ecosystem, sometimes referred to as a 'walled garden'. The product offers Apple-only platforms such as Airdrop and Facetime, which encourages people to persuade their family members and friends to buy into the same product range, facilitating use of these features, providing them with *affiliation and belonging.*

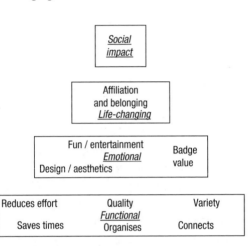

Figure 6.4 Brand value pyramid hierarchy for Apple's iPhone

Therefore, in the iPhone analysis above, it can be seen that beyond the purely functional elements – which are mere points of parity with most competitors – the iPhone delivers substantial emotional value through its emotional and life-changing elements.

EXERCISE

Using value-based pricing

A useful exercise is to numerically calculate the value your product generates. As stated earlier, this quantitative approach is more suited to some types of product than others, but the concept of comparing 'before' and 'after' is equally valid for all products.

As discussed above, there are several steps involved:

1. The first is to describe, and ideally calculate, the situation without your product being used – what is the current behaviour, what are the implications in terms of excess cost that could be saved, missed revenue opportunities or opportunity costs[9] that have been missed?

2. The second step is to recalculate the same scenario, this time with your product in use and delivering its value.

   a. For opportunities that increase sales, the right-hand column is most useful, and you may not need the middle column.

   b. For solutions that save costs, the middle column is also useful in listing the current costs (before the savings), whilst the new lower costs can be entered in the right-hand column, and a net difference calculated.

3. The overall net value created can then be calculated (the increase in value), and an appropriate portion of this value designated as the selling price.

	Scenario without product: Current behaviour	Scenario with product: New scenario
Income		
Income	i.	i.
	ii.	ii.
	iii.	iii
Costs		
Costs	i.	i.
	ii.	ii.
	iii	iii
Net value created	i.	i.
	ii.	ii.
	iii	iii
Net position		
80% retained by customer	£	£
20% of net value (e.g. price)	£	£

Guidance: The key concept in this exercise is that of the 'before' and 'after'. If you are able to describe the two scenarios and the difference between them, then you are on your way to calculating the value of your offering. It's important

▶

to keep in mind the customer's perspective in doing this exercise. Put yourself in your customer's shoes – what do they think, what value do they derive, what are their costs and opportunities? Once you've calculated the 'apple pie of value' generated you can decide how to split it up between yourself and the customer (or other stakeholders such as distributors).

A worked example is useful. In this simplified example the new scenario is one where the value is generated by a new income opportunity, but the same approach can be used for a cost-saving calculation.

Recently, I worked with a new company that was producing mushroom-growing environments for independent farmers in South Africa, 'MushMag'. These farmers typically have a small holding where they produce various crops throughout the season. However, there are times in the traditional season when the farmers are less busy, and they have opportunities to produce additional high-value crops. Mushrooms are a potentially attractive supplementary crop: they require relatively little space and high market prices are the norm, with the majority of mushrooms currently being imported into the country.

The company was selling a new technology – a mushroom growing 'tent', which is a dome made of recycled materials about a metre across with a solar cell on top to power a humidity control system inside. The control system ensures the optimal growing conditions for mushrooms. The dome comes equipped with training, as well as mycelium seeding materials and the necessary consumables.

Example economics for the typical farmer for an average year, per dome, were as follows:

■ *Labour cost to run a mushroom dome – $20*

■ *Cost of materials and consumables – $30*

■ *Value of the annual mushroom crop when sold to wholesalers – $375*

■ *Transportation cost of the crop – $5*

Therefore, assuming a prudent one-year life for the dome (it would actually last longer) then the typical farmer could earn $375, minus $20 labour cost, minus $30 materials, minus $5 transportation = $320 per dome. This was the economic value being created by this new device. Using a typical B2B percentage of 20% suggests the dome should be priced at $64.

Another way of looking at this is that the dome was producing a net 'apple pie of value' of $320, and it was being split 80:20. In fact, the production costs for the company at scale were anticipated to be about $20, so this $64 price suggested a healthy profit margin to help the company grow. In contrast, a cost-plus approach might have arrived at a figure of only $40, based on a cost of $20 plus 100% markup.

Another key benefit of the value-based method is that the value being generated can now be explained to the customer, with the case clearly laid out, and the $64 price is very reasonable for a net value (profit) portion of $320.

	Scenario without product: **Current behaviour**	Scenario with product: **New scenario**
Income		
Income	$0	+$375
Costs		
Costs	n/a	−$20 labour −$30 consumables −$5 transportation
Net value created	$0	= $320
Net position		
80% retained by customer	$0	$256
20% of net value (price)	$0	$64

KNOWING THE CUSTOMER'S REFERENCE POINT

The earlier $1,000,000 gadget example ignored competitors and substitutes, but of course customers do often make price comparisons with any available alternatives, whether they are close equivalents or broadly alternative solutions.

In fact, research shows that customers often define alternatives as *gains* or *losses* relative to a reference point or reference points, rather than to an absolute level. In other words, customers are not 'calibrated' to measure value in absolute terms, but instead need to use external reference points to establish the relative strength or weakness of a particular proposition.

To do this, customers draw upon their past experiences, their knowledge of alternatives, and perhaps most importantly, whatever other options that have presented themselves at that time.

Therefore, key questions that many businesses consider when setting price are: what are these reference points, and in what way can they influence or control the customer's reference points? If they can somehow control or influence the reference points, then the customer's calibration as to what constitutes good or poor value shifts too.

An everyday example of this is a typical restaurant. Restaurants understand that many people won't buy the cheapest or the most expensive items on the menu – thereby the restaurant has a relatively high level of control, since they alone set where these lower and upper limits lie. A wine list is a good example of this – many will not purchase the cheapest wine, and adding some much higher-priced wines, even if they never sell, may well shift the average purchase price point upwards. This so called 'magic of the middle' effect is a form of anchoring, whereby the relative position to reference points is used to help make decisions whenever there is a lack of other information, i.e. when people don't know what to choose, they decide on something in the middle. Another, if unrelated, trick that I see restaurants using is to remove the currency symbol from their price lists. Therefore $5 is shown as simply 5, or £10 is shown as 10. This practice may appear to be an attempt to look 'on trend', but some researchers suggest that the removal of the currency symbol makes the consumer less sensitive to the price – it has less of a monetary impact.

PRICE DISCOVERY BY AUCTION

There are many other ways that price discovery can occur – that is, the matching of a price to the perceived value by the customer. Good examples are auctions. There are four classic styles of auction.

ENGLISH AUCTION

In the English auction there is one seller and many buyers. The price rises as buyers bid against each other. The highest bidder wins the auction, making the purchase at a price point that reflects that they recognise more value than the other bidders (or, possibly, the other bidders had simply exhausted their available budget but would have bid higher).

> N.B. There's a phenomenon named 'winner's curse' whereby someone gets emotionally invested in winning the bidding process (a type of sunk cost) and overpays. A simple everyday example: a colleague placed a branded gift voucher of face value £220 for sale on eBay and sold it for £237. Presumably the buyer had gotten 'caught up' in the auction process.

DUTCH AUCTION

Here, there are many sellers but one buyer. The price drops as the sellers bid to win the business by offering a lower price. The winner offers the lowest price, with an obvious risk that they have underpriced and will lose money in the final reckoning.

SEALED BID AUCTION

This is similar to the English auction but there is a one-time confidential bid made by the buyers in a single time period. The winner is usually the buyer that makes the best offer.

A Dutch auction version of this process is used in many tender-based industries – although often price is only one dimension upon which the final decision is based.

DOUBLE AUCTION

In this type of auction there are many sellers and many buyers, and the auction house orchestrates the setting of prices as supply and demand changes. Examples of this type of auction include stock markets which use 'market makers' and software to aid price discovery for each exchange.

AVOIDING PRICE COMPETITION

You may be asking, what about competitors and competitive strategy? If we can undercut our competitors, it may not change demand, but we can still get the sale that they would have had. This may sometimes be true, but undercutting presumes that the products are identical, which may or may not be the case, and that customers care more about changes in headline price than other factors, such as other transaction costs associated with making a decision. However, undercutting competitors to win business is also an unfortunate way to reduce those all-important margins and start a price war leading to the weakest (and usually smallest) company going bankrupt. In fact, many companies and industries work hard to avoid price competition. Generally, price collusion is illegal. Any communication directly between competitors about setting prices or other elements of competition is strictly forbidden under US, UK and EU anti-trust laws, with severe penalties upto and including a prison sentence for anyone found guilty. However, that's not to say that companies haven't developed legal ways to avoid price competition.

Look at the following list of customer 'perks'. Do you think they are a good thing for consumers?

- **Air miles.** Air miles are given free to passengers, and when they accumulate to a sufficient level they can be redeemed for flights or other products or benefits.

- **Store loyalty cards.** These loyalty cards give points to consumers as a reward for their shopping, and these points can usually be redeemed towards other purchases, whether at the same store or another business.

- **'You can't buy cheaper' guarantees.** These guarantees serve as 'price matches'. If the consumer can find the identical product at a cheaper price somewhere else, then the retailer will match that price, ensuring the customer gets the best possible available deal.

In fact, all three of these are highly effective techniques to stop price competition. In other words, they are a way of preventing lower prices for consumers – you could say that they are actually bad for consumers in that consumers end up, on average, paying higher prices.

AIR MILES

Air miles are given free of charge in return for the price paid for a ticket on a particular airline. Once you have enough air miles from that airline, you can 'spend' them on free flights or upgrades and so on. Of course, once you start to collect air miles for one airline, it doesn't make much sense to spread your business amongst more airlines since it will delay, perhaps indefinitely, reaching the threshold of miles required to do something valuable with them (some air miles also expire over time if not used). In effect, air miles reduce the willingness of consumers to shop around for the cheapest flights, reducing the need for price competition between airlines. More sophisticated frequent flyers may collect air miles from two or three airlines and concentrate their buying power with those – however, the net effect of reducing their ability to shop around is the same.

STORE LOYALTY CARDS

Tesco was mentioned earlier and it is famous for being one of the first UK supermarkets to pioneer the introduction of store loyalty cards. In a similar way to air miles, loyalty cards allow consumers to 'earn' points in line with the amount they spend. The more they shop, the more points they earn. In this way, loyalty cards lock consumers into using just one supermarket, or sometimes consumers may share their budget over a couple of store cards, in a similar way to air miles. The added bonus of loyalty cards to the seller is that they provide the store with incredibly valuable information about the buying behaviour of the customer which can then be used to build a profile to present targeted offers and increase overall spend. In fact, the data generated by store cards is probably of greater value to the stores than the negation of potential price competition.

'YOU CAN'T BUY CHEAPER' GUARANTEES

These kinds of guarantees are promises that the shop's prices can't be beaten, and if the customer finds someone else selling the same item more cheaply, the store will match the price. This is actually a powerful form of what's called 'signalling' to other stores that actually prevents price competition. It tells competitors that any attempt to offer a lower price is futile, as the price will be matched, and no advantage will be conveyed to the discounter. It therefore discourages lowering of prices and on balance consumers end up paying more.

MAKING IT HARDER FOR CUSTOMERS TO MAKE COMPARISONS

Another way that companies try to discourage price-led competition is to make it harder for customers to 'shop around' and make direct comparisons. One way of doing this is to sell products in product bundles, whereby the fact that a product is bundled differently between competitors makes it harder for customers to make exact comparisons. The bundle doesn't have to be physical, and some elements of the bundle can include different financing arrangements or different warranty periods between different vendors. For example, if one retailer adds an additional year of warranty on all products it sells, it's hard for a typical consumer to calculate what that is worth in monetary terms, and so it makes comparisons harder.

A trick often used in consumer goods such as electronics and white goods is that a large retailer will formulate their own unique product model number (and/or stock number) for a particular product, replacing the manufacturer's standard model number, so that there is no easy way for a consumer to make a quick internet price comparison. The consumer would be required to do an in-depth analysis of features, which is unlikely to be practical for the average consumer. This tactic also makes it harder for consumers to practice 'show rooming' whereby they examine a product in a traditional store then purchase it online, usually having searched online for the cheapest supplier of the same product.

Similarly, when consumers go to buy goods from a physical store, they are often subject to the challenges of trying to compare features. Taking the example of washing machines – there are simply so many different machines, all with similar capabilities, that making a sophisticated comparison is difficult. This is not helped by retailers not displaying the same features on the information tickets across all of the machines – so a spreadsheet and a look through the machine specifications would be required to collate and capture the comparison, which is understandably difficult. This phenomenon is, of course, largely by design. When faced with an overwhelming variety of choices and conflicting units of measurement the consumer calls for a sales assistant to help, and then the retailer gains control of the sales process.

'BUY NOW PAY LATER' SERVICES

In some sectors buy-now-pay-later offers have become very popular. They often become available to consumers during an online purchase process. They are usually provided to the online retailer by a third party and essentially provide free credit to the consumer. The credit means that the consumer is able to spend more, but it also increases the likelihood of the consumer finishing the purchase and not abandoning the cart before completion. The credit services are free to the consumer – they are paid for by the retailer.

Why? Essentially the offer to 'buy now pay later' increases sales volume and reduces the need for end-of-season sales and other forms of discounting. It also subtly increases bundling, making it harder for consumers to compare the overall offer, including the credit facility, between retailers of shopping engines. It therefore offers another route to prevent price competition.

COMPANIES CHOOSE COST-INSENSITIVE CATEGORIES

Although not strictly associated with avoiding price competition, the previously highlighted McKinsey research showed that, in some cases, customers are cost sensitive to certain products, so it's important for high-growth companies to understand which category a particular product might fall within in order to make correct pricing decisions.

INCREASED DIFFERENTIATION

One final way worthy of mention here that companies use to reduce the risks of price competition is to increase differentiation. If companies make products which are sufficiently different, or significantly differentiated, then it becomes hard for customers to compare them with other products. In other words, if a given product is unique and this uniqueness is a source of value, then it's hard for price to be a prime driver to choose between it and something else.

CREATING A BUNDLE AND ADDING EMOTIONAL VALUE

I once had an opportunity to meet staff from Walt Disney's psychology unit and ask them how they viewed customer value. Such a department is sometimes tasked with maximising the value for those consumers using the Disney theme parks. The problems requiring solutions include managing the flow of traffic through the park and setting up queuing systems that don't discourage visitors, but entertain them instead.

One example of their work was regarding pricing for the log flume ride photo. As you probably know, a log flume is like a water-based roller coaster in that it lifts a boat containing visitors to the top of a ramp and then allows them to shoot down a water slide into a pool of water below. The climax of the ride is when the boat hits the pool of water, when a wave of water usually enters the front of the boat and all the passengers scream. At the same time, there's a camera that captures a photo of the passengers as they hit the water.

As the riders climb out of the boat in their somewhat soggy clothes and take the exit aisle from the ride, there's a display screen with the photo available to buy showing them as they hit the water pool. In this example, the price of the photo was $21. Perhaps understandably, given the relatively high price in an already expensive setting, the purchase rate was very low, with just a small percentage of visitors purchasing a photo.

The psychology department was asked to help. Their first proposal was to let the crowd name its own price. However, the first trial showed this to be just 99c, which was considered too low to be viable. So, another approach to value creation was taken. The price was set as $3 plus another $3 for a local charity. The price was therefore a total of $6, with half of the fee going to charity. It was deemed a great success, with a good conversion rate.

This is a good example of an organisation understanding the psychology of the customer perspective. If you've ever been to a Disney park, you'll know that the tickets to enter are not low priced, and once you are in, everything else, such as food, is also at a premium level. Therefore, the customer position is probably one of being conscious of rising costs. The new pricing of $3 plus $3 for charity meant that those who would have liked a photo, but might have baulked at the price, now had a moral-high-ground excuse to buy one. Whilst they perhaps would not have justified $6, they would justify $6 when half of it goes to a good cause. This is a great example of where increasing price over the base case can actually add value. N.B. A fairly recent innovation in theme parks has been to offer a flat price photo deal, whereby customers can pay one fee and have access to all the digital photos taken of them throughout their visit.

Other examples of creating a bundle include restaurants selling a fixed price three-course meal, and telephony and cable TV suppliers bundling TV, telephone and Internet together at a price point lower than the sum of the individual prices. These approaches all make price comparisons more difficult.

Another form of bundling is the use of loss leaders: inkjet printer manufacturers can afford to almost give away the printer, selling at marginal cost, because they will make money through the sale of electronically controlled ink cartridges. Similarly, video game console manufacturers sell the console at marginal cost because they can sell video games with very high margins and little competition once consumers are committed to the platform.

UNPROFITABLE CUSTOMERS?

Profits are usually more important than revenues. However, there are a couple of notable exceptions when this is not the case.

One is where there is a market 'land grab' – where the market is being pursued by many aggressive players and there is a sense that those who get the greatest market share quickly will be able to retain that share and generate favourable long-term positions. An example of this is the early years of the Internet, the boom years of around 1995–2000, when online companies were desperate to get users and market share in order to consolidate long-term positions. Amazon and its unusually long wait for profits is a case in point, where there was an overtly stated policy of sacrificing profits in the short term for growth and long-term market share – a strategy that appears to have worked.

Another example of profits being less important is during early product validation trials, or market validation trials. This is where a (usually technology) company wishes to get customers paying for an early stage product and, through the process of a real purchase transaction, validate there is a genuine appeal and value recognition from the market. Because of the early stage of the offering, or underlying technology, economies of scale are not yet developed, and the temporarily high costs will produce negative profits. In this case, getting early adopting customers to pay for and use the new product is more important that the profitability at that point in time.

However, in most cases, profits are more important than revenues because profits allow for reinvestment in value-adding activities which enable businesses to grow. Revenues can be part of any success story but usually revenues per se do not actually allow businesses to have higher profits, have higher dividends and have higher cash flow.

It's often said that 20% of customers contribute 80% of profits, whilst 20% of customers actually lose companies money. This is derived from the so-called Pareto characteristic. The Pareto characteristic is one where there tends to be an 80:20 distribution in many facets of business, and indeed of life.

If 20% of your customers do lose you money, then how does this happen? One way is due to the amount of time they make you and your staff waste. If they are difficult and painful to deal with, if they are slow to respond or ask for continual changes and alterations, then the sheer amount of staff time they use up makes them far less profitable than you may think.

Similarly, if they are a distraction to your business. If they are always pulling the company in different directions, asking for customisations to the product that no one else is asking for, if they want special interactions, then they can be a distraction from the day-to-day realities of scaling up a successful business formula.

High product return rates can also be a way that customers lose you money. Although the initial sales transaction may look profitable, and the accounts system says it is, when the costs of processing product returns, restocking and handling plus any subsequent 'B stock' that's being generated have been added up, it means that money is being lost. This is a common problem in mail-order businesses, particularly in areas such as clothing which can have very high return rates – especially if free-of-charge returns is the norm in the sector.

In all these cases the result will be poor margins, or even negative margins when all the true hidden costs are taken into account. And, as mentioned earlier, a problem with cost-plus pricing is that it assumes that you really know what the current true and total costs are, which is often not the case.

Unless there is a genuine strategic reason for having these loss-making customers, then the rational thing to do is to get rid of them. As painful as it sounds, and as counterintuitive as it may seem to turn away business, the fact is that without these customers you and your team will have more capacity and a more productive work environment. This extra time and energy can then be put to use in discovering and delivering on new, and hopefully more profitable, opportunities.

ENCOURAGING INTROSPECTION

Another, and possibly the biggest, problem with cost-plus pricing is that it encourages companies to look internally rather than externally. It tends to make companies introspective, thinking about their own cost structure and the margins they require to make profits. Instead, many of these businesses will be far better off looking at the external environment, looking at customers, trying to understand the customer journey much more closely, and thereby getting greater understanding about their customers and ways that they can add value to their customers lives.

Companies that use cost plus, therefore, are more introspective and less market focused. They are often not looking at what the opportunity is, but are instead focused on cost controls, running their factories or operations more effectively.

There's a stark difference between the two philosophies. One is about looking at your staff and internal processes, the other is about always increasing your understanding of the customer and the market. In most modern economies, and most new product categories, discovering customer value is one of the great potential upsides of business. Looking at these upsides and looking at new opportunities for new products, new services and new ways of making your customers lives better is an exciting way to grow businesses over not just the short term, but the medium and long term too.

IS COST-PLUS PRICING ANALYSIS EVER USEFUL?

As stated at the start of this chapter, there are industries where it is normal to have 'open books' with customers. This is where the customer contracts the supplier to show all of its costs and the supplier can apply an agreed 'markup' to generate a profit margin. In this case, the costs are transparent, and it's natural to use cost plus. It's worth noting that in cases such as contract manufacturing there's normally also an opportunity to improve costs over the duration of the contract, and this presumed cost improvement is a key source of value for the supplier, should it be able to deliver on the promise.

There are also some highly regulated industries, such as the supply of certified aerospace components. Companies buy aerospace parts, stock them and then sell the components with the necessary airworthiness certificate information at an agreed markup – designed for the supplier to cover its costs and generate a profit. The advantage of this system to safety-critical industries is that there is no incentive for stockists to take risks through sourcing cheaper components, since the customers will cover any reasonable cost with the accepted mark up in place. Indeed, the more expensive the part sourced, the higher the unit profit is for the stockist.

It's also important to say that cost-plus analysis has an important role in business, even if not in pricing. When doing business analysis and generating management accounts it's still important to understand which products make a profit and which products are relatively more or less profitable compared to others. So, from the perspective of cost accounting, budgetary controls and measurement, it's important to understand these margins and costs, and so this type of analysis has an important role to play.

In this chapter I have highlighted the importance of customer-centric thinking and customer value thinking, and also provided some insights into alternative approaches, as well as some common tactics. We will continue to build upon these themes in the next chapter and also challenge some common assumptions.

CHAPTER SUMMARY

- Traditional cost-plus pricing is no longer appropriate to meet many of today's challenges.

  - Cost plus wrongly assumes accurate cost measurement and takes no account of customer perspectives.

- Price should always be linked to customer value, which opens the door to a plethora of highly useful approaches and healthy analysis of the buying environment.

  - The competitive situation is also a useful supplementary perspective.

- It's important to know which company exchanges are integrative or distributive to understand the role of value creation and distribution.

- Meanwhile, other than a 'sanity check', cost of production should be irrelevant in pricing decisions.

- Companies routinely manipulate customer reference points and use emotional value, plus a host of other techniques, to arrive at certain pricing outcomes.

Things to consider

Value 'pie'
Are your interactions integrative or distributive? In what way?

If integrative, how can you increase the overall value pie?

If distributive, how can you claim a larger slice?

Value-based pricing
Carry out the value-based pricing exercise.
How does this compare with your current pricing decisions and strategy?

Unprofitable customers?
Which of your customers are unprofitable?
How might you be able to 'let them go'?

Chapter exercise

Using value-based pricing

CHAPTER 7

CHALLENGING PRICE ASSUMPTIONS

I f entrepreneurs and business leaders are to be able to make more appropriate pricing decisions, then they will often need to recalibrate their assumptions around pricing. These assumptions include:

■ What the sources of value are for the customer – these are often not at all obvious.

■ That customers make decisions in the same ways in which they themselves make decisions – some entrepreneurs and leaders tend to feel other people think in the same way they do, whilst more often the opposite is true, and they do not.

■ That customers are a homogenous group – whereas, in fact, customers fall into many different segments and have many different customer profiles with differing needs and propensities.

To do this recalibration, it's useful to look at new reference points and at some of the research and new science uncovering what actually underlies that customer behaviour. This is the main purpose of this chapter. We've already observed that many identically manufactured products are sold at vastly different price points, and we will build upon this observation. Some of the statements or conclusions might sound counter-intuitive or even outrageous, but it's important to get these ideas out in the open and look at the evidence.

As is so often the case when looking at sales as a subject area, not every opportunity is suitable for all high-growth companies, so you will need to gauge what is appropriate for your particular business.

Remember the price point scattergrams from Chapter 3? That chapter showed how many products command vastly different prices despite being physically and functionally identical. There's another interesting twist in the tale.

Figure 7.1 shows that many products can command very different price points by differentiating themselves in the mind of the customer. What is even more interesting is that when consumers who are buying the more expensive products from a spectrum of choices are asked how much value they are getting, they indicate they are getting more value than those customers buying at the cheaper price points. Note 'value' not 'value for money'. We'll cover this point below.

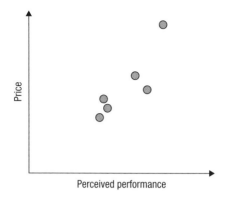

Figure 7.1 A selection of price points in a typical product category

PRICE AS A SIGNAL OF VALUE

RESEARCH SHOWS THAT HIGHER PRICES ARE USED TO IMPLY HIGHER QUALITY

Evidence suggests that customers subconsciously associate value with price. In other words, the more expensive something is, the better it is. If this were not true, then we would see many more examples where products fail to sell when they occupy higher price points because it's unlikely that they're actually proportionally better (better value for each unit of price) than the competitors – whereas what we do see is that the most expensive products in a category do well, and sometimes the most expensive product is the biggest seller.

Most customers today are short of time and use heuristics, or rules of thumb, to make decisions. One of these heuristics is to associate price with value. If you're a fairly 'regular' consumer and you take some time to examine some of the luxury goods categories or premium product categories, it's quite likely you'll be surprised by just how expensive some things are, and how much more expensive than you might appreciate. Clearly, there are customers who are buying in these various categories – and this offers us some anecdotal evidence since customers are buying and must therefore be receiving value.

Let's take the example of someone buying a handbag. One handbag might be $100, another handbag might be $500, and another might be $2,000. The fact that these products look attractive and that they are readily available suggest to the buyer that these are all viable products that are actively being bought by people. Therefore, the shortcut explanation is that the $500 dollar handbag is better than the $100 handbag, and the $2,000 handbag is better still. This conclusion is completely separate from any evidence or any analysis or whether this is true other than based on the price.

In other words, the anecdotal evidence very much suggests that consumers associate value with price, or to put it another way the higher the price, the higher the quality, the higher the value. So, is there evidence in the research to show that high prices signal high quality?

The relationship between price and quality has been explored by various researchers. Steenkamp's research[1] looked at a very large sample of 6,580 products across 413 product categories, comparing the performance and capabilities of products with their price points. The work concluded that although, overall, there was the expected broad price-performance characteristic described in Chapter 4, most correlations between price and quality were weak and it was not genuinely the case that 'you get what you pay for'. In other words, and unfortunately for consumers, manufacturers were often selling products at higher prices without offering commensurate tangible increases in quality or performance levels.

Steenkamp also suggested some useful steps that might make consumers better decision makers, such as allowing advertisers to make direct product comparisons (which is not allowed in many countries) and consumer education.

With well-differentiated or complex products, consumers are not fully certain of the quality and features of the products they buy. They are similarly often unable to make a 'quality of goods' comparison between various brands, due to the intangible value of the brand. The research finds that consumers often gather little information, even when the financial commitment involved is very substantial – people buying houses is a good example from everyday life, where the amount of effort in gathering objective data when comparing and choosing a home is not at all in proportion to the size of the purchase. Notoriously, most people are overly influenced by subjective and relatively low-cost aspects such as decor, attractive kitchens, feature-rich bathrooms, prestigious white goods and other lifestyle factors.

Also, an underlying belief remains in many cultures that 'you get what you pay for'. Therefore, consumers tend to feel that a high price is an indicator of better quality, even when the objective research shows that it's not necessarily true.

Research gives us examples of when consumers can't be fully certain of a product's true quality, including cases where the quality is highly subjective (e.g. art or fashion), for innovative goods (e.g. a new technology), or aspects that are difficult to verify prior to purchase (e.g. certificated attributes such as 'organic', and goods that have to be experienced longer term, such as bed mattresses) – consumers may in these cases turn to one or more signals, including price, to form quality perceptions.[2] Many companies therefore look to these three categories for opportunities to charge higher prices.

Verma and Gupta[3] found in their research that for a durable product, like a television, setting a price too low will actually negatively influence the quality perception of the product – they found that consumers would be reluctant to buy a low-priced brand, whilst pricing it reasonably high will give the product a high-quality image. However, they also sensibly note that the price setter should also review the competitions' price points and the target consumer segment's purchasing power.

So, has consumer buying behaviour changed over time? Eitan Gerstner concluded there was a very weak link between actual product quality and higher prices over time:[4]

'. . . Previous empirical studies on the relationship between price and quality include those of Oxenfeldt (1950), Morris and Bronson (1969), Spoles (1977), Reisz (1978, 1979) and Geistfeld (1982). All of these concluded that quality/price relations are product specific and weak in general . . .'

In other words, the research supports the idea that manufacturers sell at higher prices without necessarily always giving higher quality, and this appears to have been true at least as far back as 1950. Gerstner's own work agreed with the conclusions of the earlier mentioned studies.

It's not 100% clear whether this behaviour has increased or decreased over time, but some observers support the idea that attitudes have shifted somewhat over the last 30 years, perhaps due to an ever increasing information overload, and that high price is increasingly viewed as a proxy for high quality, even if this is not objectively always the case.

'When a product's quality is hard to assess, that's when savvy marketers tend to set prices at a high level to signal that they are selling high-quality items. This is when you should take the time to do research and try to understand what contributes to quality so that you can buy the item with the best value instead of the most expensive one.'

Utpal M. Dholakia, Rice University[5]

Additionally, according to research published by Shapiro,[6] buyers perceived that they could reduce the risk of choosing a poorer quality product by choosing a high-priced brand. Price, therefore, played an important role in indicating the quality of many products for four reasons:

1. **The ease of measurement, since price is a concrete, measurable variable:** The research paper states that for pricing, products can be seen as a series of 'cues' where the consumers' task is to evaluate the product by using these cues as a basis for making judgements about the product. Since the price is a concrete, fixed aspect for the shopper (it's not usual to expect to negotiate on price in most price settings) they trust it more than most other, less easily measured, cues. Interestingly, if the setting was one where price negotiation was the norm, then the stated price would not deliver a proxy for value in this way.

2. **Effort and satisfaction:** Consumer satisfaction with a product depends, at least in part, on the amount of effort expended by the consumer in acquiring the product – whereby the expenditure of money may be viewed by the consumer as similar to an expenditure of effort. It's said that some economists consider money as stored expended effort. Therefore, if expenditure of money is similar to expenditure of effort, and while choosing a product a consumer considers how they will feel post purchase, then the more they spend, the more they have invested, the more they will like it.

3. **Snob appeal:** This is the premium some people place on certain goods and services merely for the sake of their expensiveness. A person may prefer a more expensive model, even knowing that it is no better than a cheaper one, for the mere fact that it is more expensive. They may wish their friends and neighbours to know that they have purchased the more expensive option; they may feel that their prestige and social standing require they buy the most expensive they can possibly afford of everything.

4. **Perception of risk:** The perceived risk of losing out because of the assumed lower quality of the lower-priced product. To reduce this risk the consumer chooses a higher-priced option.

PEOPLE GENERALLY REPORT HIGHER QUALITY WHEN PAYING MORE

Consumers, therefore, are often in the situation where they don't have enough information about a certain product – what economists call a lack of perfect information. Decision making continues despite this lack of information, so consumers use shortcuts and heuristics to make judgements. This is particularly true when time is short or there is a lack of analysis and objective information. Simply put, the consumer doesn't have enough information to really tell if a product is better or not, so their mind suggests to them that the expensive product must be of a higher quality than a cheaper one.

This is similar in some ways to the powerful placebo effect, where subjects are given an inert substance by doctors but told that it is a real medicine. Taking the inert substance (usually something mundane, such as chalk) they quite remarkably enjoy a physical medicinal effect, as if they were taking an actual medication. This effect has been verified by countless medical tests. Although it's a hard-to-explain phenomenon, it suggests that the body's repair mechanism seems to be stimulated by the expectation of the 'medicine' working even when it's not present.

In their research paper 'Marketing actions can modulate neural representations of experienced pleasantness'.[7] Plassmann, O'Doherty, Shiv and Rangel from Stanford Graduate School of Business and the California Institute of Technology (CIT) tested subjects by giving them different wines to taste. They explained that a basic assumption in economics is that the pleasantness experienced from consuming a good should depend only on its intrinsic properties and on the state of the individual. Therefore, in theory, the pleasure derived from consuming a drink should depend only on the molecular composition of the drink and the level of thirst of the individual. However, their paper cites previous research where marketing actions had affected pleasantness by manipulating non-intrinsic attributes of a product – for example, knowledge of a beer's ingredients and brand can affect reported taste quality.

In their research, 20 test subjects were given five cabernet sauvignon wines to taste at five different price points of $5, $10, $35, $45 and $90 and asked to reflect on how good the wines tasted. The wines were presented in a random order. What the subjects did not know was that some of the wines were actually identical – the $5 and $45 wines were the same (the real price for this wine was $5) and the $10 and $90 wines were the same (the real price for this wine was $90).

The results were startling, even if by now not entirely surprising to you. The subjects reported that the higher priced they were told the wine was, the better they generally reported it as tasting. For the two sets of identical wines, they reported much higher pleasantness for the wine with the higher price claim (on average, approximately twice as high a rating), despite the wine being the same.

Later, when the subjects were tested again but not given the price information, they gave approximately the same rating for the two sets of identical wines – unsurprisingly, since they were indeed the same wine. So, the subjects reported very different experiences depending on the availability and positioning of the price information.

Again, with a lack of easy-to-use evidence (apparently their sense of taste did not count), the brain appears to take over and fill in blanks using price as a proxy for quality – in a sense 'if it costs more then it must be better'. The research does support the idea there may be a sense of value in providing similar offerings to customers and using price as a primary differentiator, or indeed, as mentioned before, simply making it harder for customers to make comparisons.

Deval, Mantel, Kardes and Posavac[8] suggest in their research that whilst a lower price could indicate either good value or low quality, a high price may indicate either poor value or high quality. Again, consumers usually don't have complete information and so use various strategies to fill in the gaps as they decide which products to buy. The research offers the contrasting examples that consumers may believe that *popular* products are high in quality, while also believing that *scarce* products are also high in quality. There is therefore a careful balance to consider, particularly if adopting a price leadership strategy (having lower prices) as consumers may perceive that lower prices indicate poor quality. They give an example whereby retailer J.C. Penney discovered that an advertised 'everyday low-pricing' strategy caused a reduction in brand value and alienated consumers, since their consumers believe that low prices equate to low quality.

In *Harvard Business Review* there's a piece,'Why you should charge more than you think you're worth':[9]

'. . . Author Kevin Kruse learned a lesson about understanding one's value a number of years ago from an unexpected source: someone he was trying to hire as a speaker. At the time, Kruse was running a nonprofit life sciences association, and his job was to organize the annual convention. The board had a specific person in mind for the keynote speaker, and even though Kruse had a budget of $30,000, he wasn't sure he could land the speaker, who was a New York Times best-selling author with an Ivy League doctorate and a heavy media presence.

But when Kruse called, the author quoted a shockingly low fee: $3,000. "From the outside," Kruse says, "it looked like he had all the signs of success and credibility, and we would have gladly paid *literally 10 times his asking price." As it was, Kruse wondered if the author's low fee scared a lot of people away, thinking he must be an inexperienced beginner onstage. Price is often a proxy for quality, and when you put yourself at the low end, it signals that you're unsure of your value—or the value just isn't there. Either can be alarming for prospective clients . . .'*

There's therefore a large and growing body of evidence suggesting people value more highly the things they pay more for, assuming they can afford to. This controversial point suggests that people today attach higher value to higher price, period.

In B2B at least, a possible reason for this phenomenon is that customers instinctively know that by paying the supplier more, the supplier is more likely to be around to support them in the future, to survive and to develop future products and services. Similarly, perhaps there is a feeling that paying more means being part of the 'story' of the supplier, a way of creating a deeper connection, becoming a participant in some way. Branding and intangible emotional value can be important parts of this value positioning too.

'REASSURINGLY EXPENSIVE'

There's a fun example from UK popular culture between 1991 and 2002: a hit advertising campaign by the beer brand Stella Artois. The brand developed a large and prolific TV advertising campaign around the slogan 'Reassuringly expensive'. Many of the adverts positioned the beer as a high-end luxury product with a price tag to match. This was despite the fact that it had previously occupied a regular position in the market with respect to other export strength lagers. By positioning the beer as expensive, it followed that the product must be both of the highest quality and something to aspire to drink – presumably to show that the drinker is a successful person. According to Adbrands.net:

'. . . In the US and Canada, a similar concept was used but with a different slogan of "Perfection has its price" . . .'

The commercial and its message was a great success, boosting sales during the period in which it ran, creating for Stella a position as the UK's best-selling premium lager; interestingly, with a broad appeal to all sociodemographic segments, not just the affluent.[10] The adverts also received more awards than any other campaign in 2002, including the coveted advertising industry Cannes Lion.[11]

TESTING PRICE POINTS WITH CUSTOMERS

A useful and sophisticated technique is to test price points with real customers. This has the advantages of trying out actual buying behaviour in a real-world setting with real customers who can then indicate their underlying behaviours.

Another example from *Harvard Business Review* shows how companies can use pricing tests to uncover market dynamics and interpret real customer behaviours.[12]

> '... Joe Listro, Olay's R&D manager, explains how it went. "We started to test the new Olay product at premium price points of $12.99 to $18.99 and got very different results," he says. "At $12.99, there was a positive response and a reasonably good rate of purchase intent. But most who signalled a desire to buy at $12.99 were mass shoppers. Very few department store shoppers were interested at that price point. Basically, we were trading people up from within the channel.
>
> At $15.99, purchase intent dropped dramatically.
>
> At $18.99, it went back up again—way up. So $12.99 was really good, $15.99 not so good, $18.99 great."
>
> The team learned that at $18.99, consumers were crossing over from prestige department and specialty stores to buy Olay in discount, drug, and grocery stores. That price point sent exactly the right message. For the department store shopper, the product was a great value but still credibly expensive. For the mass shopper, the premium price signified that the product must be considerably better than anything else on the shelf. In contrast, $15.99 was in no-man's land—for a mass shopper, expensive without signalling differentiation, and for a prestige shopper, not expensive enough ...'

This is a great example of many cases in the real world, where there is a 'sweet spot' for a higher price, where customers respond very positively and actually increase their propensity to buy. This idea can be counter-intuitive to the business manager and is also hard to predict. Testing the market is, therefore, one of the best approaches to uncovering such sweet spots.

EXERCISE

Design a market experiment

Market experiments are very powerful ways of answering questions which can otherwise be difficult to resolve. For example, A/B testing is an easy way of using the market to answer a difficult question, e.g. 'Which of two marketing email designs is most likely to be successful?'

A simple A/B test would apply each design to a small sample of customers and measure the results for both samples. The more successful 'winner' would then be used for the greater data set. By contrast, the traditional way of answering this question would have been far more complex and far less reliable – analysing the contents of the two emails and attempting to match them to the audience profile to predict which would be better received.

The design of a market experiment is similar to the experimental process that many of us experienced in science classes at school:

1. *Set the objective – what is the objective of the experiment?*
2. *Design the method – what are the steps required to carry out the experiment? How much budget do you have available for the experiment?*
3. *Record the results – what results or measurements have been gathered?*
4. *Conclusions/What we discovered – what answers has the experiment produced?*

The Olay example above showed that a price test can uncover hidden customer preferences and types of value recognition, but you can design an experiment to answer many different types of questions.

You can use the table below to design your own experiment:

	Fill out the column below:	Notes:
Set the objective	*i.*	*What is the objective of the experiment?*
Design the method	*i.* *ii.* *iii.* *iv.* *v.*	*What are the steps required to carry out the experiment and meet the objective?* *How much budget do you have available?*

▶

Record the results	i. ii. iii. iv. v.	How will you set up a measurement process? What results or measurements have been gathered?
Conclusions/ What we discovered		What answers has the experiment produced?

Guidance: An internet search will furnish various examples of companies carrying out market tests. But failing all else, a test can be arranged around any of the classic 4 Ps of marketing – Price (try a different price point), Place (try a new distribution method), Product (tweak the product messaging or attributes) and Promotion (test a different advertising method), whereby any of the elements can be adjusted and a result measured. N.B. Running a single-market test can be very valuable, but establishing a system or process to resource and run frequent tests can be a hugely beneficial facility to help any business scale and grow, by removing levels of uncertainty about customer behaviour and preferences.

BRAIN SCANS INDICATE RATIONAL IRRATIONALITY

Let's go back to the Stanford/CIT research mentioned earlier: 'Marketing actions can modulate neural representations of experienced pleasantness'.[13] You may recall that subjects were tested by giving each of them five wines to taste at five different price points in random order, and asked to reflect on how good the wines tasted. The subjects didn't know that two pairs of the wines were actually identical – the $5 and $45 wines were the same (real price $5) and the $10 and $90 wines were the same (real price $90). When the subjects were not given the price information, they were unable to differentiate between the $5 and $45 wines and then again the $10 and $90 wines, and gave them similar scores – unsurprisingly, since the wines were the same. By contrast, when they were told the wine price points, they reported greater pleasantness for the higher price wines. Similar phenomena have been verified many times by different researchers. However, the next aspect in this research is even more interesting and innovative.

The researchers tested the subjects using functional magnetic resonance imaging (fMRI) and electroencephalography (EEG), scanning the subjects' brains whilst they tasted the wines, including the two wine pairings that, contrary to reality, they believed to be different and sold at different prices. The remarkable results showed that for the two pairings of identical wines, the higher price point not only increases the subjective reports of flavour pleasantness, but also increases blood-oxygen-level-dependent activity in the medial orbitofrontal cortex – an area of the brain that is widely thought to encode for actual experienced pleasantness.

Figure 7.2(a) – Liking: the subjects' overall liking of the wines increased with price. The $5 and $45 wines were the same wine – however, the score is approximately twice for the higher price point. Similarly, the $10 and $90 wines were the same – the score is twice for the higher price point.

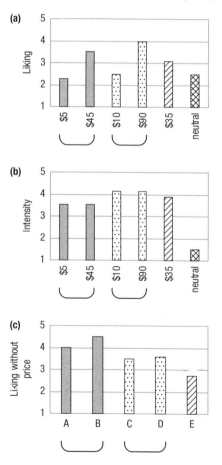

Figure 7.2 Wine feedback scores. even though the $5 and $45 dollar wines were actually the same, as were the $10 and $90 dollar wines, subjects preferred the one with the higher price tag

Figure 7.2(b) – Intensity: it's interesting that the subjects ranked the $5 and $45 wines as having the same intensity – since they were, of course, the same wine. Similarly, with the $10 and £90 wines, which were also identical.

Figure 7.2(c) – Liking without price info: in contrast to 7.2(a), in a second tasting without price information supplied to them, subjects' 'Liking' scores ranked A and B roughly the same and C and D roughly the same – each pair was indeed identical.

Figure 7.3 shows the activity in the medial orbitofrontal cortex for the two identical wine pairings during the course of the tasting experience. The top chart shows higher activity for the '$45 wine' from the point of tasting onwards, despite being the same wine as the '$5 wine'. The bottom chart shows a similar result for the $90 and $10 wines – again, the activity in the brain is higher, in this case much higher, for the $90 wine despite it being the same as the $10 wine.

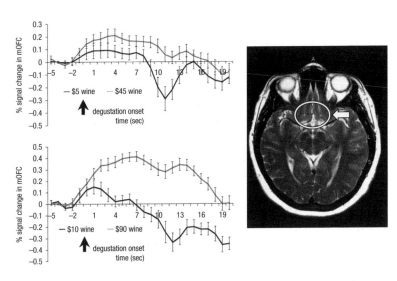

Figure 7.3 The physical reward from both wines went up when the stated price was higher

The remarkable results show that the *actual processes* occurring in the brain were different for the higher price points despite the wine being the same. In other words, the subjects were genuinely getting more physical reward from the same wine whenever they were told it was sold at the higher price points. This is a much more fundamental and important point than the subjects simply reporting that the wine tasted better because it was described as more expensive. Since there's an increase in physical reward with higher prices, perhaps irrational decision making has a rational element after all?

Development of the MRI machine is credited to Peter Mansfield, who was a professor at Nottingham University, and Paul Lauterbur and their work in the 1970s. They were later recognised for the amazing benefits that their innovation created for humankind, being awarded the 2003 Nobel Prize in Physiology or Medicine. Increasingly, there is a recognition that technologies such as fMRI and EEG offer a more reliable way to diagnose and measure consumer response to different purchase decisions and/or advertisements.[14] These tests can be carried out in small groups and then the results can be more widely deployed in the market or used in the marketeer's decision making.

A key advantage of measuring actual physical responses is that it avoids some of the problems of traditional market research in which participants incorrectly report their preferences or reactions to certain things (because they are not truly in touch with the decisions that they make), or participants are unwilling to express their true feelings to researchers (they tend to express what they feel they are expected to say due to social pressures rather than what they really think).

The subject of priming is covered elsewhere in this book, but the general unreliability of traditional market research is perhaps most famously captured by the New Coke episode. In the 1980s Coca-Cola had been losing marketshare to a very aggressive Pepsi. One of the devices that Pepsi had used to good effect was the so-called 'Pepsi Challenge'.

In the challenge cola drinkers were asked to blind taste Coke and Pepsi in front of TV cameras. As often as not, the Coke advocate would choose Pepsi rather than Coke as the drink they preferred in the blind taste test. For TV advertising, die-hard Coke customers were shown taking the blind taste test and being shocked when they discovered they had chosen Pepsi. Coca-Cola became so concerned about this apparent result that they reformulated the recipe for Coca-Cola to create the so-called 'New Coke' – a new recipe that could match or even beat Pepsi in the same blind trial. The new recipe was said to be somewhat sweeter and could outperform Pepsi in the environs of the taste challenge.

New Coke was duly launched and became an instant failure. Existing Coke customers were outraged because they wanted the original Coke that they expected. This furore caused Coca-Cola to then hurriedly re-release the so-called 'Coke Classic'. In time, New Coke quietly exited stage left, never to be seen again, and Coke Classic became Coke once again.

The fallout from this and the unwelcome exposure of the previously highly admired decision making at Coca-Cola caused the senior board of Coca-Cola to come out and publicly apologise for the whole episode.

There were many points of failure in the affair, although ultimately it did have an unexpected silver lining. In terms of failures, there were several technical research failures: there was no recognition that taking a single sip of a drink is not the same as consuming a whole serving of a drink, where the taste builds on the palette over the duration of the serving. There was also no recognition that Coke customers do not consume their beverages in an artificial environment in front of an audience, but rather at home or in a restaurant. There was a failure to accept that consumers loyal to a product did not wish to be dictated to as to when the product should drastically change.

More fundamentally, there was a failure to recognise that the nuances of the taste of any cola product are far less important than the writing on the side of the packaging, i.e. the brand and messaging. Customers bought Coke primarily because of the emotional value delivered by the brand, and their relationship with this brand over time, so taking away the brands made the Pepsi challenge taste test entirely meaningless in terms of real-world value. Otherwise, surely everyone would be drinking generic cola products at a fraction of the price.

There was one silver lining for Coke. As the company flip-flopped around with multiple versions of the same product for sale, they noticed something surprising: total sales went up. Further trials showed that the more different types of Coke they offered to the market, the more sales increased. It appears that a proliferation of products increases consumption in some way. That perhaps explains why today there are more than ten types of different Coke brands available to buy.[15]

THE PARIS WINE TASTING

The Paris Wine Tasting of 1976 is an important event in the history of wine,[16] but also an interesting one for those studying human decision making. At the time, French wine was unquestionably considered the best in the world, with many famous and prestigious chateau names representing the pinnacle of wine making.

A wine tasting event was organised in Paris in that year by a British wine merchant, with 11 famous French wine tasters charged with tasting a selection of French and Californian wines in order to compare and rank them. However, the tasting was to be blind, i.e. the wine tasters would not know which wine they were tasting. This was considered the fairest way to compare the wines. If you've read the previous section on the New Coke episode you may be able to guess what happened next.

The judges tasted a selection of some of the most prestigious red (Cabernet Sauvignon) and white (Chardonnay) wines from California and France and entered their scores out of 20 into a ballot which was submitted for scoring.

The results were shocking at the time – a Californian wine was ranked #1 in both the red and white wine categories. The French wine industry and the French tasters were horrified by the result. It was considered a great scandal and it has remained a divisive result ever since.

Follow-up wine tastings were held with the same wines, this time in the USA, in 1978, and, again, a US wine ranked #1 in both categories. Another test was held with the same red wines in the French Culinary Institute (New York) in 1986 with the same result.

Many detractors have criticised the way the tasting was conducted and scored. Irrespective of whether one nation's wine is better than the others (and some have pointed out that New World wines tend to be more approachable than their Old World cousins and this may explain the dominant result) we can reapply at least two of the lessons from New Coke.

First, in the real customer world no one consumes these wines as a single taste amongst 10 or 20 wines, so the testing mechanism and the way that the tasting palette evolves was somewhat flawed in design. Second, and more fundamentally, taking the label away from a premium-branded historic wine removes much of the meaning of the product. As we saw with New Coke and with the examples in this chapter, the brain's 'consumption' of the brand, its heritage and other messages are just as important and 'real' as consumption of the actual physical attributes, such as taste.

PEOPLE AREN'T RATIONAL DECISION MAKERS

From much of research it can be seen that consumers aren't rational, despite them usually thinking of themselves as rational beings. Many entrepreneurs and business leaders make the same mistake about their customers.

In *Thinking, Fast and Slow*[17] Daniel Kahneman explains that whilst the brain's conscious System 2 thinks it is in control, it's actually the faster acting subconscious System 1 that does much of the decision making. The System 2 then tells itself why it made the decision, often retrospectively justifying the choice made by System 1.

Therefore, the instinctive System 1 makes many of the decisions, and only subsequent analysis will show that these decisions are actually less than logical, or poorly considered in purely logical terms.

Many of the examples cited in the published research are in the B2C arena, where consumer goods interact with customer decision making. However, similarly, B2B also isn't as rational as is often assumed, since human beings are still involved in the process. Value is usually more qualitative, interpretive and subjective, than it is quantitative and objective. B2B might try to be more rational, more process based, but people are still involved, and people are emotional animals.

Also, most managers and businesspeople (in common with much of the population) are trained by advertising from an early age to think along the lines that product companies want them to, and this also changes their decision making. In B2B, the decision makers are assumed to choose the optimal option to meet the procurement needs, but often these procurement processes are seen to have been refashioned to suit the needs of the procurement decision makers – usually in a way to make their lives easier, an understandable human trait. This opens the door to the canny marketeer or price setter.

In classical economics, frameworks would be formulated to predict the decision making of the rational consumer as free decision makers in a free market. Thinking of a restaurant example, customers would make rational choices based on the value of different items on the menu, their health or dietary needs and their level of hunger requiring a certain portion size. But instead, it's become understood that most restaurant customers decide what to eat based on the feelings they experience when they think about certain foods. So powerful an idea is this that feelings and emotional value have, in many ways, become the frontier of marketing over the last 30 years, primarily through the development of brand messaging.

WHAT IS EMOTIONAL VALUE?

One of the reasons that customers pay a premium for a particular product is due to emotional value. This emotional value is sometimes realised or referred to as *brand value.* But what is emotional value?

An intangible element, emotional value in today's products makes up a significant portion of the total offering. Emotional value is the reward an individual or organisation gets from affiliating itself with a particular type of purchase decision. For example, in general terms, people buy Apple products and other premium products because of the way it makes them feel. This is a useful way to define emotional products – emotional products make people feel better about themselves, about the decision they've made in an emotional context.

This is in contrast to functional products, or staple products, which are bought simply to achieve some sort of task and are therefore subject to more scrutiny for value for money for competitive comparisons – because it's easier to compare things that are purely functional rather than those things which have an emotional content.

If we think about luxury goods, almost all of these have large elements of emotional value. This emotional value may be represented by the brand in question, or it may be otherwise implicit in the purchase decision. If we think of Mont Blanc pens, Aston Martin motor cars, Luis Vuitton handbags, then all of these have an essential common purpose of making the buyer feeling better about themselves and so on.

Business leaders have found that one of the best ways that they can increase their margins and further differentiate themselves from any competition is by finding ways of adding and delivering emotional value through their products. This in turn can lead to a more successful outcome in terms of making price comparison shopping more difficult for customers, hooking into the all-important decision-making processes of the customer's brain.

We saw this in Chapter 4 too, when we highlighted the different price points being occupied by essentially the same products. As we saw, the only difference between those products were the packaging, the branding and the associated emotional value.

Thinking back to the ideas of distributive and integrative transactions of Chapter 5, injecting enhanced emotional value is one of the key ways that sellers create a bigger apple pie of value, making what could have been a difficult 'win lose' distributive exchange into a bigger and 'win win' integrative transaction.

WHAT CUSTOMERS LOOK FOR IS VALUE, NOT VALUE FOR MONEY

We've established that price is proportional to quality in the minds of many customers. However, what is it that the customer actually wants? It's tempting to think that all customers are rational machines, actively doing value for money analysis and comparing products with alternatives to look for the 'sweet spot' for value for money.

However, unsurprisingly, the real case is that people again use shortcuts to think about value, more than they think about value for money. Let's take another example to explain this. Let's think about a budget laptop available for $400, a laptop at $1,000, and a laptop at $2,000.

Laptop A	$400
Laptop B	$1,000
Laptop C	$2,000

We can map the actual capabilities against price. In this case all three run the same operating system, so the main difference is the amount of memory and the speed, plus improved weight, webcam and screen.

	$400	$1,000	$3,000
Word processing	***	***	***
Remote working	**	**	***
Spreadsheets	***	***	***
Email	***	***	***
Web browsing	***	***	***
Wireless Internet	***	***	***
Viewing movies	**	***	***
Battery life	**	***	***
Weight	**	***	***

We can represent this as Figure 7.4, showing the total score for each of the laptops, plus another option – which is to have no laptop, when none of the capabilities are available.

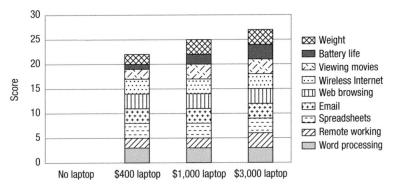

Figure 7.4 Summary of scores: the more expensive laptops are somewhat more capable

If we compare the capabilities of these three laptops, are there really any major differences? The reality is that the cheapest $400 laptop is capable of doing virtually everything that the most expensive one can, despite a price multiple of 7.5.

Similarly, we can show the change in total score as we progress from the cheapest option (no laptop) to the $400 laptop, from the $400 laptop to the $1,000 laptop and from the $1,000 laptop to the $3,000 laptop. This is shown in Figure 7.5.

It's probably fairly obvious, but in terms of increasing value, going from zero to getting a basic but capable laptop is a vastly more useful step than taking the additional steps up in value. Looking at this highly rational analysis, the basic $400 laptop is therefore, by far and away, the best value for money. Of course, the analysis has not included the intangible aspects, such as the brand name and the expectation of how the physical look and feel of the devices will change the ownership experience, all of which contribute to large amounts of emotional value.

If consumers were really looking for value for money, then, even in affluent Western economies, the vast majority of products sold would be at the lowest price points of their categories or segments since that is where lies the most 'bangs per buck'. This is usually not the case. However, what should be becoming clearer is that customers do not look for rational logical value for money, *even if they think they do*; what they actually look for is value up to a price they can afford, which is a different thing altogether and usually this value contains a large emotional component. It can also be said that value is that thing which gives them the information they require to make a purchase decision.

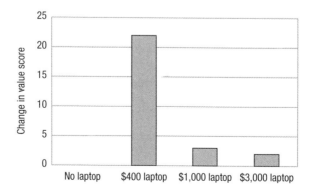

Figure 7.5 Change in value score from previous category: the biggest increase in value is from 'No laptop' to '$400 laptop'

Hopefully it's a little clearer now that finding value is a key objective of customers, as opposed to straight forward value for money, and *finding out what value means to the customer is one of the key objectives of any entrepreneur, or business leader.*

A successful restauranteur with a chain of restaurants reflects on how they set price with regard to three factors:

'. . . We set price with regard to three factors: first, and most importantly, there's perceived value, then there's market pricing and finally there's a 25% cost check.

Perceived value is all about creating restaurant products and services which are experiential, which have strong points of difference and give the customers extra value. This may include preparing some dishes at the table, which introduces a touch of theatre, preparing dishes with great visual appeal and creating an environment or ambiance that customers enjoy. It's also about points of difference and supplying something that is unique and memorable.

Market pricing is important because every restaurant operates in its own local market, and each local market is different. A restaurant in one town will have different costs but also different market prices for eating out depending on the local demographics. We therefore assess what competitor offers are like and how they are priced to make sure that we are competitive in any easy comparison points that customers might make – common comparisons they might make include the price of a pint of beer or a basic glass of wine, so it's important to have price competitive points available to allow for favourable comparisons. For items that are not benchmarked, or not easily compared, we can be more aggressive on price.

The final point is 25% cost – we check that the materials cost of any of our dishes are not higher than 25% of our selling price. Otherwise, we need to increase the selling price, reduce the portion size to support our finances or cancel the item altogether.

We have found that there are customers who simply want low prices and then we have customers who are far less cost sensitive. We focus on attracting and signalling to the latter.

Our menus are designed to provide customers with a range of options and cover a range of price points to do this. Many customers will not purchase the least expensive thing on the menu, perhaps due to concerns that it will be too small or not satisfying, so we can position prices accordingly. We include some premium price points, particularly in easily stored items such as wine, to allow those who wish to, to 'splash out'.

Market conditions in large cities are strong, but in smaller towns, whilst Thursday to Sunday are strong, Monday to Wednesday remain a challenge. Price discounting remains common in the industry for these days of the week in these smaller cities. We therefore offer on-sell and upsell options through our front-of-house staff to help encourage people to receive a bit extra. These deals focus on crowd pleasing dishes with high margins.'

THE RISE OF CUSTOMER EXPERIENCE (CX)

An increasingly globally connected economy means that both buyers and sellers have greatly increased choice. It means that more information is freely available making it easier to make price comparisons, leading to increasing levels of damaging price competition. It also means there's an increasing speed of commoditisation as product functions converge and become standardised.

We are in the middle of the information revolution and this has had a profound effect on some industries. Traditionally, buyers did not have information they required to make optimal choices and sellers tended to be in the driving seat. Today, with the passing of this information asymmetry and the greater transparency produced by data availability, the traditional business model has become outdated in many industries. As a poker analogy, it would be like trying to play the game with an open hand, when everyone else can see your cards. This idea is similar to the efficient market model in economics, where if a market is truly efficient then marginal profits are driven towards zero.

In the broader context, some businesses are moving from distributive to integrative models, where relationships are becoming less transactional, less based on price discovery and more about value discovery – and particularly how to add additional value. In this context, one of the most interesting developments over the last decade has been the rising importance of customer experience, sometimes called CX, and this has been one of the principle ways in which high-growth companies have sought to differentiate themselves and compete without putting pressure on price, particularly in industries where offerings are similar – where companies are all offering essentially the same thing.

Research published by *Harvard Business Review*[18] looked at 6,000 mergers and acquisitions worldwide between 2003 and 2013. It established that as a percentage of the total enterprise value (the value of the company), customer value increased significantly over the ten-year period, doubling from approximately 9% to 18%. In a way, this can be thought of as customer loyalty. Meanwhile, the same metric showed that the more obtuse physical attributes of the brand (such as trademarks, product names and mastheads) halved over the same period. The research therefore highlights an alternative view on the rising importance of emotional value and relationship, particularly in the context of recruiting and retaining customers.

So, what is customer experience? The customer experience is the qualitative aspect of interactions an individual has with a company, its products or services at any point in time. This means it covers the pre-purchase process, the purchase process itself and the post-purchase reflection too. Importantly, it's qualitative rather than quantitative, therefore it's open to perception by the individual through their sensory and also their psychological faculties. CX is therefore said to be less about what the product or service does, but more about how it does it. CX is all about individuals, because companies aren't sentient but are a collection, or collective, of individuals who are all emotional animals.

In short, CX is the customer's (or potential customer's) perception of how your business treats them. CX is therefore often an important way of adding emotional value to a product or service offering. In some industries customers prefer what is easiest, or what feels most personally rewarding at a price they can afford, rather than what a rational choice would suggest.

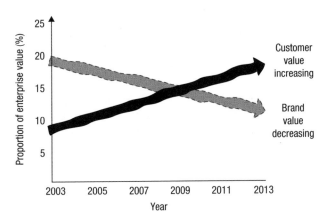

Figure 7.6 The declining value of brands and the rise of customer relationships[19]

Economists have traditionally developed tools to help explain customer decision making in difficult or complex environments, when there may be many criteria. These, so called, multi-attribute models of decision making take a view on the various aspects and sometimes apply a weighting to help reach a decision. However, these rational models of decision making do not always account for actual customer behaviour. CX tends to suggest that customers choose what is easiest, or most pleasurable, rather than what is most rational.

APPLE INC. AS AN EXAMPLE

Once again, Apple is a great example of a business finding out what customers value and providing them with it, and with great financial success to boot. At the time of writing, Apple has a cash pile, which is to say a store of cash and cash equivalents, of over $250,000,000,000. This is said to be more than three times than that of the US Federal Reserve. The fact that it has such a huge cash pile is testament to its premium pricing, margins and business strategies.[20]

Apple offers only premium products, often the most expensive product in any of the categories in which it operates. This premium pricing strategy has created customers who value Apple for its easy-to-use technology, and also for its avant-garde styling, minimalist fashion and customer service. Apple products are not necessarily the most powerful or the most capable, although they certainly have products at the upper end of performance in their product lines. But what Apple is really good at is creating emotional value for customers and for charging premium prices to reinforce this.

So, the fact that Apple charges such a price premium over what might be expected for a typical branded manufacturer, is one reason why its margins are so healthy, and why it has accumulated large profits, and this is overtly demonstrated by its huge cash pile. This is, of course, all enabled and supported by the strength of its value proposition and sustainable competitive advantage.

WANT TO SPEND MORE?

Consumer marketing offers us many examples of how companies are extending the range of their pricing towards premium levels.

Generations Y and Z (born after 1981) are the most brand-conscious generations ever. They have been brought up in an unprecedented environment of branded consumer products which rely on deeply rooted emotional value drivers. Think about the success of the iPhone, Facebook and Instagram's roles using photos and videos in communications. Think modern networked console games, branded coffee stores and sports clothing brands.

The range of prices in many product categories has increased enormously. Could anyone have predicted 25 years ago that normal consumers would indulge in products which command a 5 to 10 times multiple over what might otherwise be considered the 'best value for money' in their category?

Examples include price points beyond £1,000 for a tablet computer – which is more than a 10 times multiple over the least expensive device of a similar size from a big brand supplier; £1,500 on a 'consumer' DSLR – a 5 times multiple; £4,000 on a mountain bike – 20 times more than a basic model. Looking around, all of this price diversity is absolutely normal today.

The point is not that consumerism has gone mad, but that all of the above products deliver far more emotional value than they do functional value, and this is the 'new normal', an environment that younger generations, and marketeers, understand innately.

THE NEED TO REWIRE THE BRAIN

Reflections by SME business leaders on the process of starting a new business sometimes highlight how the experience has shaped their thinking. When they start a business, they often put together an offering, launch it, at some point customers turn down that offer, the offer is then improved until finally they get a sale. Now they've become cautious, they have found it's not always easy to get sales. A natural response to this is to keep prices low in the belief that it will help encourage sales.

There's a similar story when larger businesses launch new products. Such a launch is a journey into the unknown. Overwhelmingly, evidence suggests that the majority of these product launches either fail outright or do not meet their original objectives. Previous experiences within any successful company will therefore include many failures, so there's an element of caution, of reducing risks to the company and to the managers involved. Lowering prices may appear to be a hedge against market refusal, although the problems associated with this have been discussed in this book.

There's a need to re-wire brains that have gone through these experiences. Many SME owners have said that the experience of getting from zero to $1,000,000 in sales can take several years and a lot of heartache.

The more difficult aspects of this journey tend to leave the entrepreneur feeling somewhat cautious and keen not to waste any effort involved in bringing customers on board, so they believe it's best to keep prices low. This reticence to charge higher prices is part of the cognitive bias that I mentioned in Chapter 1 around the confidence in the value proposition and the fear of not gaining enough business to pay all the overheads and other associated costs.

Anecdotal evidence suggests that those who are able to put aside the caution created by that initial journey, or by previous failures, are more open to entrepreneurial thinking, including the important opportunities that come with pursuing premium price positions and higher margins.

It's worth noting that the bumpy start-up experience mentioned above is not true for all high-growth companies. Some happen to develop, or find themselves in a situation, where the products or services 'fly off the shelves', whether this is down to good judgement or blind luck. This usually occurs in new markets that are either growing fast, or older markets that are very large and going through a period of innovation. These experiences lead such individuals to have a very different perspective. These types of business are very different in the challenges of how to scale up and grow, perhaps more focused on operational scaling. In the next chapters we'll consider what high growth rates bring to companies.

CHAPTER SUMMARY

- Customers think they're rational decision makers, and many business leaders blithely accept this.

- Yet research suggests otherwise – value is more qualitative and subjective than it is quantitative and objective.

- The multiple price points of bottled water and how companies have sought new ways of adding value to – and charging more for – the same H_2O molecule is a great illustration.

- Extensive research shows that higher prices are a powerful signal of value and quality.

- Many price differences can be attributed purely to emotional value, which is delivered via branding, messaging and packaging.

- Underpricing makes even less sense in a world where people attach a higher value to a higher price

▶

Things to consider

Challenging price points

In what progressive and useful ways can you challenge price points by changing your assumptions?

What have you discovered about customer value recognition?

What experiments can you run to make more discoveries?

What don't you yet know?

What aspects of sales and pricing in your business do you not yet fully understand, but would save you time and/or money to know before scaling up existing processes?

How can you run experiments to find the answers?

CHAPTER 8

UNLOCKING GROWTH: USING THE INTERNAL RATE OF RETURN

arlier, in Chapter 5, there was a discussion on working capital, why it's so important to company growth and how price has a large influence upon it. Now, I'd like to highlight something even more important: the company's internal rate of return.

GETTING A RETURN ON INVESTMENT

If you had a spare £1,000 and wished to invest it, what kind of interest rate would you hope to get? If you give it to a bank, the chances are the interest rate would be low, probably a few percentage points.

By contrast, what's the annual return you get for every £1,000 you keep and reinvest in growing a business? The answer is what's known as the company's internal rate of return. For a *growth* business it's probably 25%. For a technology start-up business it's probably 40% and could be 50% or higher. By contrast, for a large company, such as those listed on a main stock exchange, it will often be 10% to 14%. As you can see, the earlier stage, faster growing, smaller companies usually offer the highest rates of return.

That means that for every penny you can invest (or reinvest) in your business you will get between 20%–50% annual compound growth in value – or rate of return – each and every year. It effectively works like an interest rate. If you think about it, that's an incredible increase in value.

It shouldn't surprise us that early-stage or high-growth businesses create these sorts of return. After all, it's not unusual to witness or be involved with growing businesses which increase their sales by 30%, 80% and over 100% per year, and if the sales are growing at that pace, then the profits and 'value' will hopefully follow (assuming management ensure that margins, and so on, remain healthy). By way of example, Inc. Magazine[1] publishes an annual list of high-growth businesses that have been chosen from a wide variety of sectors – it includes many examples of companies that have grown their sales by over 10,000% over three years, which is a compound rate of 364% in each of those years.

We can also look at data for high-growth businesses that were early stage but are now reporting their results in the public domain (usually as a company with publicly traded shares). Since their data is readily available, we can do some simple but useful analysis.

A simple search on finance websites tells us that Amazon in 2019 was worth about $900 billion. Looking at its valuation about 14 years earlier it was a 'mere' $26 billion. That's an annual compound increase in value of roughly 29% per year over 14 years, impressive for what was already by then a very large company. Doing a similar analysis for the period of 23 years from 1997 to 2020, the growth rate in value is 38% per year. If we look at the first 10 years (from 1997 to 2007) it's higher still, as you might expect considering smaller companies can usually grow faster, at 46% each year. Remember though, even in 1997 Amazon was a large corporation. If we were able to see data for the earlier period, we'd see even higher rates. For example, there's some data available that suggests that the sales growth rate (as opposed to company value) was an average 1,100% per year from 1995 to 1997.

Similarly, Facebook increased in value at 28% per year from 2012 to 2020. In the first portion of that period, from 2012 to 2017, it was 36% per year. There's not much data from when it was a much earlier stage company, but the top line sales growth from 2006 to 2011 was an average 137% each year.

Amazon and Facebook are in the so-called 'unicorn' club. That's not to say that every high-growth early stage company needs to have the potential to become a unicorn to be successful, particularly with all the additional complexities such companies require – such as raising investment capital and managing public market expectations. However, these public domain examples are useful to us to look at here to underline the growth and return rates available from your own business, whether it's a microbusiness or an international company.

THE BANK WITH 25% INTEREST RATES

If a bank you trusted offered you a 25% interest rate on deposits, what would you do? You would probably rush to put every penny you could into that bank account, wouldn't you? Would it surprise you, therefore, that a high-growth company is essentially offering the same opportunity, albeit with a certain level of risk? Every penny a high-growth company creates through profits and then reinvests in itself can give these exciting levels of internal rates of return.

We've already stated that high-growth businesses generate internal rates of return of 25%, 40% or even over 50%. That means that for every pound they reinvest, the value of that pound increases by that percentage each year. This is the fundamental reason that venture capitalists invest in early stage businesses (through venture capital investments) and high-growth larger businesses (through private equity investments), and why share-owning management teams of successful high-growth businesses can become very wealthy.

There is of course a higher element of risk in any business than in a national bank (at least, usually, although there have been a few notable bank collapses in the last century), and the value in an early stage business is not liquid, or even visible, in the way it is in a bank statement, but the internal rates of return for successful early stage and growing companies are large. Therefore, a business should maximise the amount of capital that it can usefully invest into the business because it is getting this amazing rate of return.

Which means, if you can generate more profit and more cash, and invest that back into the business, that money will earn high compound interest rates. We've already seen that if you manage your price effectively then you can expect to generate more profit and more cash, which will help you unleash the potential of your business.

Here is an example: £1,000 in a bank every year at a 2% compound interest rate and the same £1,000 for an early stage company at 35% internal rate of return.

As you can see in Figure 8.1, the company scenario returns a total after five years that is a factor of over three times higher than the bank, or over 300%. This is the power of the compounding of value over the time period.

And, if we keep it going for another five years the difference is a factor of 12 (see Figure 8.2).

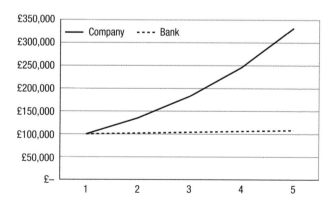

Figure 8.1 Comparison of company and bank investment returns, five years

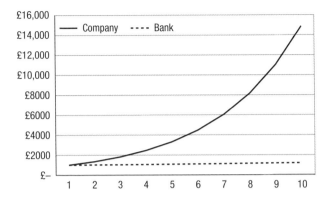

Figure 8.2 Comparison of company and bank investment returns, ten years

COMPARISON TO A PASSIVE COMPANY

We've compared the investment returns of an early stage company to a bank account and seen the different results from investing in them. This time let's compare two companies, where one company generates and reinvests the extra cash produced from higher prices, and one equally profitable company that does not reinvest and either leaves the money in the bank or pays it out as dividends, and see how vastly different the outcomes are after even a few years.

As we can see in Figure 8.3, the company that effectively reinvests into sales, staff training, product development and operations puts that money to work, compared to the company that made no use of the funds, perhaps

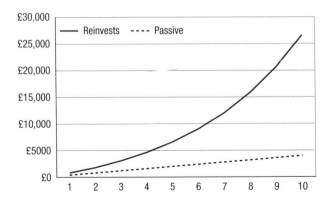

Figure 8.3 Cumulative company value

leaving it languishing in a bank. The company that reinvested the capital has a far higher growth curve and is three times more valuable over the period.

It should be fairly self-evident, but it's worth pointing out that there are two general uses for profits. They can go back into growing the business, and thereby be put to 'work', or they can be taken out of use. Putting the money to work by investing in an activity in which you or the company are the expert, can yield high returns. This can also offset the need to raise external investment capital. If you are generating more profit by raising your prices, then this virtuous circle is further reinforced, and the growth opportunity can be maximised.

MAKING THE REINVESTMENT, BUILDING SUSTAINABLE COMPETITIVE ADVANTAGE

When I say reinvestment, what do I mean? Well, reinvestment in your business is concerned with finding out where to put your limited resources so that you can have sustainable and effective growth in the business. The exact areas of investment will be different for different companies in different sectors, for different business models and for companies at difference stages of growth.

However, the common areas include scaling sales processes, staff recruitment, staff training and development, developing new technologies, other forms of product development, operational capabilities and investment in working capital (finished product stock, raw materials, creditors/debtors or accounts receivable/payable). Also possibly included here could be capital investment (capex/capital expenditure) in new machinery and assets – although finance specialists in most countries offer separate direct financing options for such capital assets, where the asset can be sold to a finance company in return for a monthly lease payment, making the cash available for spending elsewhere.

Earlier in the book, I stated that the long-term competitiveness of a company is safest when it is based on sustainable competitive advantages and a cohesive strategy. A sustainable competitive strategy means that the company can prosper, even in the face of substantial competition and this is strongly linked to pursuing an effective strategy. The source for developing a cohesive and successful strategy is usually one of the two approaches below.

1. **The resource-based strategy:** The first strategy approach is internally derived, it develops a special capability within a company's

operational base. This can be predicated on some form of unique technology that the company owns, or it could be a unique capability which has been developed that gives the company its competitive edge. Either way, the resource is also hard (and/or expensive) for a competitor to replicate. Therefore, the resource-based strategy is to develop something within the organisation that produces an output that is both valuable to the customer and is hard to replicate.

The resource could be an asset that gives the product or service its innovative features – often this innovation is based on a technological breakthrough that could be legally protected by patents or other forms of intellectual property frameworks, making them impossible to duplicate. The resource could also be based on design capabilities, where the superior design delivers a market advantage – whether this is achieved through a unique technology or hiring and retaining the best design personnel. This strategy can also support a form of product differentiation leadership, with products that have superior features and technology.

Examples of resource-based strategies include Illumina, which is a leader in the genome sequencing market. Illumina developed valuable and patent-protected technologies which supported and helped protect both the capabilities of its product range and its leading market position. When Illumina acquired Cambridge-based Solexa in 2007 (and its new next-generation sequencing technology that was supported by a bundle of protective patents), Illumina ensured that it would retain leadership in the genome sequencing space.

Another example, this time of a different type of unique resource, is The Body Shop and its founder Anita Roddick. The Body Shop was founded in 1976 in Brighton. Anita Roddick was a strong and visible advocate for the business and its approach of using ethically sourced and naturally based ingredients from around the world. Highly visible to the public across many forums, Anita Roddick became the unique resource of The Body Shop, and her public profile and campaigning on many issues became a key source of competitive advantage for the company, its values and its products.

---

2. **The market-based approach:** The second main approach for strategic development is related to identifying and executing new market opportunities. If new market opportunities can be identified or predicted, then the first to capitalise on these opportunities is often the one who benefits the most. The strategic advantage comes about

from the organisational design, with a rapid 'sensing' mechanism within the organisation that can quickly spot market opportunities and then an equally fast and efficient capability to carry out the actions required to effectively fulfil these opportunities.

The company may have no other unique advantages over the competition, but the ability to spot and execute market opportunities fast means that it achieves first mover advantages, allowing it to be commercially successful as a pipeline of new opportunities emerge.

Examples of market-based strategies include Zara, who makes use of its information systems and responsive supply chain. The information systems allow Zara to quickly spot which products are selling well and then it uses its agile supply chain to quickly replenish products. This is in contrast to most apparel companies, whose popular products normally sell out and cannot be replenished by supply chains fast enough to meet the demand before trends change again. The clothing industry traditionally works in three-month cycles, and four collections per year, so Zara's strategy is based on market sensing and speed of response.

Other examples of market-based strategies are the large food retailers, who use vast amount of data, often from their point-of-sale systems supplemented by the tracking provided by their loyalty card schemes, to see emerging product trends and opportunities. They then reconfigure their physical sales spaces to take advantage of those opportunities whilst leveraging their supply chains to provide the necessary products. If something is starting to sell well, they can give premium promotional positions to that product, and ensure supply keeps up with demand.

It's worth mentioning a related idea that combines to some extent the two classical approaches above: that of dynamic capabilities.[2] These are defined as the ability to adapt rapidly to changing environments by building or reconfiguring both internal and external competencies. This should not be thought of as an attempt to do both the resource-based and market-based approaches at once, which would not be advisable. Instead, dynamic capabilities take into account the longitudinal aspect – how the dynamics of the company situation change over time, and how the resource- and market-based views can interrelate over various stages, as a company and its strategy evolve over time.

THE UNIQUE SELLING PROPOSITION (USP)

Sometimes also known as the customer value proposition, the USP is simply the thing that the company does, which customers value enough to pay money for, that is somehow different (and hopefully superior in some way) from its competitors.

The USP is therefore a critical part of any business's capabilities. The ability to articulate the USP is important, both to lead to effective development strategies and also to be able to explain to the customer as part of marketing communications for why they should buy something, i.e. why it is valuable to them.

Any company that has not developed a strong USP will struggle to compete in most industries, at best being relegated to being a so-called 'me too', or generic offering, most likely competing on a low price – which we've already established as being difficult, unless that is the overt strategy.

So, if the USP is the thing that the company provides which the customer values, then it's a very useful exercise to analyse a company's USP. A simple but powerful USP analysis technique is shown below.

The USP analysis should be carried out for each product or service and repeated for each segment that the product or service is sold into. Different segments may recognise different types of value, even from the same product, so it's important to do the analysis for each and every segment.

The analysis also differs depending on whether the product or service is operating in an existing market category or a new one. This is a key point of failure for many innovative companies, where they believe themselves to be competing with traditional providers, when in fact they are not, since their offering is brand new and not offered by others.

Furthermore, for innovative products creating a brand new market, rather than 'there is no competition', as many innovative companies are prone to claiming, the competition is in fact the current buying behaviour, i.e. the prospective customer ignores the new innovative offering and continues with whatever their current behaviour is. In other words, when many innovations are introduced, potential customers simply 'shrug', or 'walk on by', and continue with their current behaviour, doing nothing differently.

There are then three main questions to answer, each in comparison to either competitors, or to customers simply 'doing nothing':

1. What value or benefits are you offering?
2. What makes you unique and better than the competition?
3. Why will someone buy from you?

This is summarised in the matrix in Figure 8.4.

	1. For existing products Compared to competition	2. For new product categories Compared to 'doing nothing'
(1) What value or benefits are you offering?	1 _____ 2 _____ 3 _____	1 _____ 2 _____ 3 _____
(2) What makes you unique and better? (Differentiation)	1 _____ 2 _____ 3 _____	1 Start with substitutes, and what 'pain'? 2 _____ 3 _____
(3) Why will someone buy from you?	1 _____ 2 _____ 3 _____ 4 _____	1 How are you making the customer's world better? 2 _____ 3 _____ 4 _____

Figure 8.4 USP analysis matrix

EXERCISE

Doing the USP analysis

A. *Decide whether you are doing the analysis for a product that competes in an existing market with similar competitors (in which case use Column 1 and base your answers on the competition), or whether you have an innovative product or service without direct equivalents (in which case use Column 2 and base your answers on what changes the customer from their current behaviour and what prevents them from doing something new).*

B. *Choose a product (or service) and a customer segment.*

C. *There are then three main questions to answer:*

1. *What value or benefits are you offering?*

   Answer from the customer's perspective – try to imagine being the customer. What is it that the company is providing that the customer values?

2. *What makes you unique and better than the competition?*

   In what ways are you different, or differentiated, from competitors' offerings? And, are these points of difference valuable to customers, and if so, in what way?

N.B. For Column 2, since there are no existing competitors, start with a comparison to substitutes and ask 'What "pain" are you fixing?', 'Is this "pain" big enough to change behaviour?' and 'How are you making the customer's world better'?

3. *Why will someone buy from you?*

   The third question may seem like a repeat of some of the elements of the first two questions, but is designed to really press the analyst, to get to the root of what drives customer decision making and why a customer should choose your offering in particular.

An example for each of Column 1 and Column 2 are shown below. (N.B. they are unsegmented for our ease of use, whereas to do the exercise formally we would pick one customer segment and be more focused.)

Example: Apple iPhone (unsegmented)

Existing product category

1. For existing products
Compared to competition

What value or benefits
are you offering?

1. Easy-to-use technology
2. Great user experience
3. Ecosystem of 'apps'

What makes you
unique and better?
(Differentiation)

1. Games + music + App Store
2. Easy-to-use technology, for
   'non-techies'
3. Attractive + prestigious
4. Snob appeal
5. Most expensive in category
6. Safe 'walled garden'
7. Brand emotional value
8. Apple products work
   together

Why will someone
buy from you?

1. Makes them feel special
2. To 'show off'
3. Be part of a community
4. To use technology that they
   otherwise could not master
5. Integrate games and music
   and apps

Example: Segway (unsegmented)

New product category
= There is no direct competition

2. For new product categories
Compared to customer 'doing nothing' new

What value or benefits
are you offering?

1. Electric transportation
2. Easy to store and park
3. High viewing position
4. Unique look and feel

What makes you
unique and better?
(Differentiation)

1. Easier than cycling
2. Easier than walking
3. 'Hop on, hop off'
4. Being futuristic

Why will someone buy
from you?

1. To stand out + look different
2. To have fun in public spaces
3. To avoid walking
4. To be an early adopter

Guidance: If you have not asked these types of questions before, or haven't the information to answer the questions, then starting with a SWOT analysis (Strengths, Weaknesses, Opportunities, Threat) can be very helpful, as can be doing a comparison table of product features and benefits between yourself and competitors.

INVESTMENT CAPITAL

The enticing ideas in this chapter around growth and the high potential rates of return offered by successful innovative businesses are some of the reasons why the entrepreneurially minded are so excited by the opportunity and potential offered by high-growth companies.

Venture capitalists and angel investors are interested in these businesses for similar reasons. The prospect and potential of earning 20%, 30% or even 50% annual compound returns is financially exciting and an important element of innovation and the driving of growth. It's quite routine for venture capitalists and other investors to invest on the basis of 30% to 50% annual rates of return on their money in growing businesses.

A typical professional investor puts money into a portfolio of companies. Of ten investments, typically two or three go well, four or five may 'break even' and two or three may be a total loss. The investments that go well, therefore, have to be able to pay for those which are losses, hence the need for attractive high-return opportunities to invest in.

One of the key success factors for any professional investors is in aligning the interests of the management team with those of the investor. The more aligned these interests are, the more likely that the management and the investor can have a favourable outcome. This is often achieved through equity ownership and bonus schemes. Alignment of interests can be true for your business too. If you are the business owner or a shareholder, then your interests are clear. If you are the entrepreneurially minded manager of a larger corporation then hopefully you have some other form of alignment to encourage you in the same way.

Through applying this same approach, you are, in a way, becoming your own investor – by generating the kind of profit levels that can meet your cash needs as you grow. Different types of business have different types of working capital models, but if you have higher prices, supporting and supported by a strong USP, then cash management and getting good use out of your internal rate of return is far easier and more effective. Many growing businesses do need to raise investment capital to help with working capital requirements. Whilst some companies are fortunate to avoid this need due to the working capital structure they happen to have (such as a positive working capital model) – whether this is through luck or design – those that have the need for investment and bank funding can in any case reduce this requirement through higher prices, leading to better cash flow.

It's far easier to be successful in all of these scenarios if you have applied smart pricing – finding a price which is high enough to support good gross margins and good net margins, leading to good levels of profitability and cash flow, which in turn enable you to drive the growth in your business through reinvestment. The thinking and rationale behind the higher price are also likely to focus the company on differentiation (what makes you different and better than your competitors) and most importantly on building customer value: what it is, and what it means. It also promotes customer-centric thinking in terms of what this means to the customer.

In the next chapter we'll explore this further and ask the useful question: can you double your price?

CHAPTER SUMMARY

■ In stark contrast to a typical bank account, a growing early stage business typically has a compounding internal rate of return of 20–50% a year.

■ Creating and reinvesting profits allows the building of a stronger value proposition and sustainable competitive advantage.

    ■ As well as having a substantial impact on company value generation over even a short period of time.

Things to consider

Market
Is your product in an existing category or creating new category with new buying behaviour?

In what way?

USP
For every segment you serve:

1. What value or benefit are you offering?

2. What makes you unique and better than the competition?

3. Why will someone buy from you? What's your USP?

Chapter exercise

Doing the USP analysis

CHAPTER 9

WHAT HAPPENS IF YOU DOUBLE YOUR PRICE?

DOUBLE YOUR PRICE: PRICE AS AN AGENT OF GROWTH

We've talked about how incredibly important price is to delivering profits, and also about the great rate of return that reinvesting profits can achieve in a high-growth company. However, sometimes companies are 'shy' about raising prices, or reluctant to challenge their own assumptions about their current price points. A challenge I therefore often give to companies I work with is, 'Can you test what happens if you double your price?'

More precisely, this means one of the following two options:

1. Is there a safe test, a ring-fenced experiment perhaps, that you can conduct to see what happens if you actually double your price?

   Or, if this is simply not possible,

2. Can you run a thought experiment to see what you would need to do to feel comfortable doubling your price?

I've been fortunate to deliver thoughts on pricing to audiences comprising CEOs, business owners and senior managers. It's always a pleasure when someone in the audience confirms they have already followed a similar path of price development. Sometimes, someone gets in contact many months later to report success from a new enhanced pricing experiment. The experiment sometimes provides a realisation that the company had been chronically underpricing, other times that a higher price could be used to generate superior financial returns that could in turn be reinvested to improve the value proposition of the company. Virtually never do they report they learnt nothing of value from the experiment.

OPTION 1: RUN A SAFE MARKET TEST TO DOUBLE YOUR PRICE

Many companies that have found a suitable way to successfully carry out this option are surprised and, ultimately, transformed by the results, since it offers a route to achieve the vastly higher profit margins we saw in Chapter 3. This in turn enables the reinvestment returns we saw in Chapter 7.

If you accept that you probably have the same cognitive bias as other companies when it comes to price (i.e. you don't know what you don't know), then the only real way to find out what the market will pay is by

> *An example of a company that tried out Option 1 was an attendee of a growth programme for high-potential companies run by Nottingham University.*
>
> *The company in question provided video production services. At the time, it had grown strongly in the East Midlands and was looking to grow in other parts of the UK, including London. Having attended the training programme, the CEO decided to double the company price list for any new clients inside the M25 – essentially doubling the prices for London.*
>
> *Having done this, the team was astonished to find that the new price made no difference to the lead-to-sales conversion rate in this market – the rate remained roughly constant. However, of course, it had an enormous effect on profits and the generation of cash that could be reinvested in the business.*
>
> *What the team realised is that it had been chronically underpricing. With the new pricing level in the London market they were no longer appealing to the 'bottom feeding' price-sensitive customers, but, having moved up the value ladder, they were now seen as credible to premium customers, who had regarded them as being too cheap to be credible before. With this revelation they raised prices progressively (not quite so radically) in all other territories. As a direct result of this, the company tripled its employees in just a few years.*

getting the market to tell you – and one of the best ways to do this is by running a test.

It's important to recognise the notion of safety in exercising this idea. Companies that do this exercise skilfully act in a safe manner. They do not recklessly 'roll the dice' in uncontrolled price doubling across their business and wait to see what happens. Instead, they carry out a controlled experiment and monitor the results carefully. It could be as simple as doubling the price list when entering a new market or specific territory. Or it could be launching a parallel offering at a much higher price point and observing what happens. More options are highlighted in the following exercise.

If the market reacts positively to a different price point, a compelling mandate is provided to the management team to find out what is going on. Uncovering the reasons for this good result further helps the business understand the customer perspective. Some companies have done these exercises and increased their prices by 100%, even 300%. Other companies have decided that 25%–50% increases are more suitable for their circumstances.

EXERCISE

Double your price

There are several easy ways companies carry out the Option 1 experiment in a 'ring-fenced' safe manner:

1. ***When entering a new market:*** *New markets offer opportunities for expansion but they also offer a fresh start, a chance to do something different. New markets also are, by definition, separate from the existing business, so changes and risks here can be separated from the existing business activities. This can offer a safe ring-fenced environment to try something different with pricing.*

   As tempting as it can be to take a 'cookie cutter' approach to new markets, copying whatever is being done in the current market, it's often the case that each new market has slightly different needs anyway. Taking a fresh approach can include a doubling of price, and the lessons learnt can then be reviewed from a broader context.

   If it doesn't work out, the existing business has not been harmed and it's always easy enough to bring prices down, although do this progressively. It could be 200% wasn't the correct answer, but 150% (i.e. a 50% increase) or even 125% (a 25% increase) of the old price will still transform the margins of any business and enable enhanced reinvestment.

2. ***When launching a new product:*** *Similarly, a new product is an opportunity for a fresh start. A chance to try something novel. Price offers a great opportunity to start traction at heightened levels of profitability and a chance to learn from the experience to see if it indicates previously unexploited opportunities for the existing products too. The idea of price skimming versus penetration pricing is useful when introducing new products.*

3. ***By increasing average transaction value:*** *There are some occasions where companies find that the headline price, or sticker price, has significant signalling value and can't be increased safely. This may be, for example, where the customer buying behaviour uses the headline price as a filter in some way, perhaps as a first qualification step which leads to a fuller business discussion. In these cases, large increases to the headline price may exclude the company from the subsequent sales process.*

   In these cases, companies find that it's still possible to raise, or even double, price through focusing on the overall transaction value. Although the headline price may be too sensitive to change because it needs to be pegged to certain levels, companies have found that the overall transaction can still be increased by adopting a range of tactics such as pricing menus, price runways, bundling, on-selling, upselling and so on. A full explanation of these techniques and others can be found in Chapter 11 – along with an example of how Range Rover offers options which, taken together, almost double the price of a vehicle.

4. ***By creating parallel products:*** *We saw earlier how some companies sell essentially identical products at varying price points. Companies do this by launching a parallel product that is largely the same as their existing one(s) but with particular features or benefits either accentuated or focused. Doing this, they perhaps reference the research that highlights how some customers actually feel a need to pay more – they get more value from paying more, whether it's reassurance or an imputed stamp of quality. An interesting aspect of this experiment is how additional price points frame and direct customer decision making. The following is an example for an industrial products company:*

A company had developed a product range based on an innovative materials technology. One of the unusual characteristics of the technology was that it could be used to manufacture products that could potentially be sold to solve problems in three entirely different markets – to replace metallic bronze products in the marine sector, to replace plastic products in the chemical sector and to replace stainless steel alloys in the energy sector. For various reasons, including the different traditional materials used in the different sectors, those markets had three completely different price point expectations. The most attractive of the three markets supported a price point three times higher than the least attractive market.

The company had its origins in serving the least attractive market. It wanted to enter the new markets and enjoy the higher prices, but couldn't, because its existing sector (which was paying the bills) wouldn't support those higher price points. The obvious thing to do was to turn the current product range into three product ranges and sell each at a different price point. This would separate the three markets and potentially stop price shopping between the different price points. In essence, comparing prices across sectors would become much harder for customers. The two higher price points would also help legitimise the products and new technology in those sectors, the current price otherwise being seen as too cheap to be credible.

▶

To do this, the company created two new product lines, with new brand names. For each, new values and messages were created that were associated with the new target sector, as well as a new and higher price point. The company recognised that it was also important to make them look different and to communicate why they were suited to a particular sector (and not any other sector). Finally, since the existing product range had features that could be associated with all three markets, the company 'unbundled' (or deemphasised) some of the stated product features for each new range if these were not applicable to the new target market.

This strategy was successful and enabled them to pursue the more attractive opportunities and raise their average price substantially.

This example had three sectors with different competitors. Recall that in the water scattergrams and other examples earlier in the book the only differences between products selling at vastly different prices were the branding and packaging. This suggests that for some product categories the physical product can essentially be the same if the brand and messaging are different. Of course, the brand and messaging that accompany the product are very much part of the bundled offering, part of the value proposition, and can be invested in and changed accordingly.

OPTION 2: DO THE THOUGHT EXPERIMENT

If it's not possible to do the actual experiment, then a thought experiment can also be very worthwhile. This is because it quickly forces the company team to both raise its expectations of what is possible and also take on a customer-centric thinking position about value recognition – what opportunities there are to increase value and differentiation.

What changes in your value offering would make you comfortable in doubling the price? It's an interesting thought.

OPTION 3: RAISING EXISTING PRICES IN EXISTING OPERATIONS

There is a third route available to companies, and that's to raise prices in existing operations, whether speculatively or as a matter of survival. It's a little riskier than the two options above in that it directly affects the existing business, but it can be done successfully. This can be tried out progressively or as a step change. The correct choice between progressive or step increases will depend on the dynamics of your business and your risk appetite.

When raising prices in existing markets it's important to think about how you are communicating this to the market. If there are existing customers who enjoy buying at a discount price, then they are clearly going to be disappointed at an unexplained price increase and may complain. This is to be expected and you need to be prepared for this. If there are potential customers who have not been buying from you because the offer was seen as being too cheap (and therefore poor quality), then there's a need to reposition the brand and the offer to support the higher price. Sometimes the complaint is not about the magnitude of the price rise – it can be explained why prices are increasing – but about the timing. If budgets have already been set, then it can cause a lot of administrative pain for a client to accommodate a change in cost – in which case backloading any changes to a later date could help accommodate the increase, perhaps in return for a multi-year deal. Remember, raising prices well is also about how you frame the offer for the market, and what you include as part of the value proposition – this includes the messaging and the 'wrapper' – in the sense of how it's delivered. Once more, remember the examples from Chapter 3 where the messaging and the packaging are the key differentiators for enormous price differences.

For more ideas on how companies raise prices for scenarios such as those above please refer to Chapter 10, where companies' strategies for price increases will be looked at in more detail.

BEING TOO CHEAP IS WORSE THAN BEING TOO EXPENSIVE

Cast your mind back to the research in Chapter 7 that told us that being cheap is often seen as being of poor quality. Companies don't attract premium clients when they are too cheap, consequently they don't generate the healthy profits required to reinvest in staff, products and processes.

As I've mentioned earlier, even without doing the actual market price doubling experiment, doing a thought experiment is very useful and thought provoking as it forces teams to consider, perhaps for the first time, what would need to happen in order to double their price. Through this process, there is a healthy re-examination of the value principles at play in the customer's world.

CHRONIC UNDERPRICING

The value gained from this exercise, particularly for SMEs and early stage businesses, sometimes stems from the problem of chronic underpricing. Anecdotal evidence has indicated that many SMEs, perhaps a majority, tend to underprice. Doing the price doubling challenge, either as a carefully constructed safe and ring-fenced experiment or as a thought experiment, forces the company and its team to grapple with the idea of exactly what it is that customers value and how this value is represented in their product or service.

In the case of doing the actual experiment, the market itself will provide you with the answer through its buying behaviour, indicating whether the pricing level is right, and as to whether you are underpricing or not.

If doing the thought experiment of how to justify a doubling of price, then the management team really needs to think very hard about what it is that they would have to do to augment or change the offering to support such a price increase. Once again, this is a very healthy analysis to undertake in any case and can often lead to insights about how to further differentiate the product or add further value, or produce a hierarchy of price points across which the offering can be placed.

PRICE AS VALUE

Again, as the research in Chapter 7 demonstrated, many customers use price as an indicator of value, where value means higher quality, lower risk and so on. When these customers see a high price there's a cognitive bias to assume that it's a higher value and better performing product compared to one inhabiting a lower price point, at least until further information is brought to bear. There's also the increase in physical reward in the brain related to price levels. Therefore, this kind of research result suggests to companies that the act of repositioning a product with double the price, even without making any other changes, can deliver this extra value to the customer, purely by virtue of the fact that it has a higher price point.

This may seem counter-intuitive, but research also seems to highlight that there are many companies which use premium pricing strategies successfully, especially in industries where it's difficult for customers to make analytical comparisons between offerings. We've also mentioned companies such as Apple which uses premium pricing as a core aspect of its product range, despite the fact that much of the product range is roughly equivalent in functional terms to direct competitors usually selling at a lower price point. Apple similarly operates in its own ecosystem – whereby making comparisons to other platforms becomes more difficult.

Some companies do engage in a continuous process of product appraisal and improvements. However, most businesses look at how they can supply their product or service more effectively and in higher volumes. The examination that we are talking about in this chapter, however, is around the price point, something that companies do not routinely revisit and re-examine. Therefore, one of the key sources of value from this sort of exercise is in learning to look at the world differently, understanding customer value dynamics differently, and doing this frequently enough so that any opportunities to increase price by increasing customer value is recognised and taken advantage of.

It's also important to note that the purpose of this exercise, of asking how we can test, what will happen if we double our price, or what do we need to do to justify doubling our price, is not necessarily to try to achieve a price increase of 100%. As stated in the exercise above, for some companies the appropriate price increase might be 40%, for others it might be 200%. The purpose of the exercise and the framing of the question is really to explore the sources of value to the customer and establish what it is that your business should be doing to ensure it can grow successfully, at a suitable reinvestment level and maximise its true potential. This is good for both you and for your customers.

A price evolution case study – *A UK-based marketing agency*

In the early days of this fast-growing search engine optimisation (SEO) and digital marketing company, the organisation didn't have sophisticated methods to decide what to charge customers. They observed they were winning customers' business and the company headcount was going up to support the new activity. Things therefore 'felt good' and the business was assumed to be succeeding, although it was also observed that everyone was overly busy. This was perhaps due to their initial price – which was creating relatively low margins, which meant they were unable to fully resource, or even adequately resource, the work they were winning.

Nonetheless they were able to deliver a high volume, low margin product. They sold a seven-hour work slot but usually ended up working eight hours. This put a lot of additional pressure on the staff.

When the company came to implement the 'double your price' exercise, they incrementally increased their pricing on all new business by 20% and again by 10% over an 18-month period. At this point some customers complained, and there were some difficult discussions with clients. However, the company realised that these were in fact the wrong type of clients, and that they would be better off without them. These were a minority of cases, and most clients accepted the changes, which were accompanied by an explanation that the higher fees would result in a superior service offering.

Another tranche of increases followed soon, with an additional 5%, then another 3% then 3%, which took the price to essentially 50% higher than the initial price.

At the same time, and perhaps surprisingly, the conversion rates were increasing – perhaps in part due to the business now looking bigger and more in line with its price, due to the extra money being reinvested back into the company. This investment, in turn, led to various industry awards and prizes.

The next commercial strategy development was the attention paid to customer experience, the designing of a customer experience that not only met but exceeded client expectations. The company also shifted its approach from variable units of work to selling a fixed amount of time and money with a negotiable level of deliverables attached to that. They had effectively standardised their sales unit.

They also found that some of their staff were now too junior to properly manage client relationships and so additional investment went into this area to ensure alignment between the ability to deliver and the customer needs. This included the development of an account management function within the organisation with a more strategic overview. The focus was on service and relationships, and especially on providing much better communications with and to clients, which led to better outcomes for everyone. The price increased by another 20% over this period.

During the entire period of five years, the company grew from a team of two individuals to a team of over 60. The use of higher pricing as a way of exploring and adding value to the business was essential to the success of the growth story.

CUSTOMER DECISION-MAKING LANDSCAPE

To find ways to help customers evaluate and frame value, it's useful to look into their world and assess their decision-making landscape. For example, customers may perceive high transaction costs or emotional costs associated with their current buying choices, and if you can identify these, you can find ways to help them overcome these costs.

A useful framework to do this analysis is represented by the set of customer decision-making scales, or seesaw, shown in Figure 9.1. In

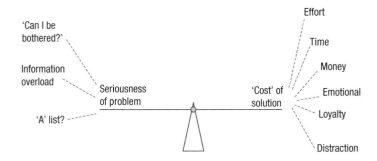

Figure 9.1 Customers 'weigh up' purchases

making purchase decisions, particularly for new or alternative products, customers weigh up the seriousness of the problem against the cost of the solution.

In this analysis, seriousness of the problem can include the simple 'hassle factor' – can customers be bothered to engage with the problem you are trying to solve? Are they under information overload, so any new information you are sending their way is likely to be ignored? Does the issue or problem that you are addressing appear on their 'priority A' list of issues that they are concerned with, and perhaps actively looking to solve? Or, is it on their B list or, even worse, their C list, in which case what can do you do to shift it to their A list? If it remains on their B or C list, the chances are they will never get around to addressing it.

On the other side of the equation, what are the costs that the customer perceives? Not just money, this includes the effort they are required to expend in pursuing the discussion and opportunity, the amount of time that such effort would take and whether they feel they have any spare time and energy. It's also the emotional cost of changing something – it could be that they have some loyalty, or trust in the current solution, and this would need to be displaced. There's also the distraction factor – how much is the issue a distraction to their important personal objectives? Although 'cost' is not necessarily about the monetary aspect, it could be – if so, what else on the cost side can you reduce to raise the price and still swing the 'scales'? If the net result, even with a higher price, is a lower overall cost, then it could be a compelling improvement.

EXERCISE

Map the customer decision-making landscape

For your company, think about a particular client prospect and fill out the following fields. If you struggle to answer some of the questions, then try to work out what you need to do to find out the necessary answers – this may take some useful research or some further discussions with customers.

Seriousness of the problem (the more serious the better)

1. *How motivated is the customer to make this change? Why is this the case?*

2. *How often does the customer hear from similar or competitive providers? How can you make the decision easy for them, avoiding information overload?*

3. *Is the issue on their 'priority A' list? If not, what is on it, and what can you do to promote the position of the issue you are addressing?*

'Cost' of the solution (the lower the overall cost the better)

1. *What is the effort you are asking the customer to expend in order to take the next step? How can you reduce this?*

2. *How much time will it take for them to complete their role? Can you reduce this?*

3. *How important is the price of the transaction? How about the timing or structure of the monetary flow – perhaps the timing is more important than the amount, or multiple instalments are greatly preferred? What reference points are they using in establishing their decision making?*

4. *What emotional factors are there in their decision making? Are they someone who likes changes and seeks it out, or are they conservative?*

5. *Are they loyal in some way to what they currently do? Are there existing supplier relationships in place that would need to be displaced?*

6. *To what extent do they feel that your solution is a distraction to their pursuing their priorities? Are there ways that the importance of the transaction can be reinforced?*

Guidance: Understanding the decision-making landscape from within which your customers make decisions can be hugely valuable. In using the scales to do the exercise, you are seeking to understand the relative strengths or weaknesses of your offering compared to 'where your customer lives', i.e. compared to the other issues that they are facing or feelings that they have. The results can help us increase perceived value, as well as finding ways to simply make it easier for the customer to make purchases.

CHAPTER SUMMARY

- Is there a safe test, a ring-fenced experiment perhaps, that you can conduct to see what happens if you actually double your price?

  - When entering a new market?
  - When launching a new product?
  - By increasing average transaction value?
  - By creating parallel products?

- Alternately, can you run a thought experiment to see what you would need to do to feel comfortable doubling your price?

- Companies that carry out such a test are often surprised – and, more importantly, positively transformed by the acceptance of higher prices and the results they produce.

- Even a price doubling thought experiment can force companies to see things very differently, providing a healthy re-examination of the value principles at play in the customer's world

Things to consider

Double your price	Customer decision making
Is there a safe way to test what happens if you double your price?	How do customers weigh up decisions?
e.g. entering a new market, launching a new product, creating a parallel product	Map their decision-making process.
	e.g effort, time, money, emotions, loyalty, distraction

Chapter exercise

1. *Double your price*
2. *Map the customer decision-making landscape*

CHAPTER 10

UNDERSTANDING COGNITIVE BIAS AND BEHAVIOUR

There's a fascinating area of management science, psychology and behavioural economics that concerns itself with cognitive biases and how these affect the way that people make decisions. It's a large and interesting subject, and it's useful for us to take a brief look at it to see how it helps us better understand some of the driving influences around pricing and general buyer behaviour. This science is the 'bread and butter' of how entities in B2C markets make decisions, and it has an important role in B2B markets too.

Additionally, as a consumer, you can also use some of these ideas to better defend yourself against common tactics and, in doing so, get yourself a better deal.

As a reminder, I stated earlier that chronic underpricing was largely due to a cognitive bias, or more accurately, based upon several cognitive biases. One part of this body of work is regarding framing and priming. I want to highlight this area to aid our understanding of how customers view price, because it gives us insights as to how companies set and raise prices.

Many of these biases exist because of the human evolutionary story. In particular, the need of our ancestors for a fast, reflexive way of making decisions.

This is skilfully explained by Daniel Kahneman in his book Thinking, Fast and Slow,[1] where he speaks of System 1 and System 2 decision-making units in the human brain sharing the business of how we make decisions. System 1 is fast, and makes the bulk of our decisions by using rules of thumb, and with shortcuts rooted in our deep history. System 2 is slower and more logical, but is hostage to the strong presence of System 1. In our evolutionary history these systems had positive roles to play, but they are now available to be used by politicians, the media and also marketers to maximise their own value, not necessarily that of the consumer. Although System 1 is doing much of the decision making, System 2 thinks it's in control – essentially our conscious mind retrospectively creates reasons why certain decisions are made, but these are usually incorrect since the subconscious mind made the original choice. It's been long known that many customers can't adequately explain why or how they buy – and their stated reasons don't hold up to scrutiny.

CUSTOMERS FALL PREY TO BEHAVIOURAL HEURISTICS AND BIASES

Many tests over several decades have demonstrated that consumers are surprisingly irrational in making decisions. However, they don't think they are. This is an important point. Most people, when asked, will say that they take due care in making purchase decisions. All the evidence proves the opposite is usually true for the majority of people.

Therefore, we can conclude that most of the following content falls 'below the radar' of most buyers. They are subject to these influences, but are probably not aware of them, unless they have been trained to specifically look for them.

PRIMING BIAS

Priming is the non-conscious perception of information where the first information is given a greater weighting over information that follows later. In other words, the first information changes the way that the subsequent information is perceived. First is more important than second, is more important than third or fourth etc.

A simple example from Philip Graves's book *Consumer.ology*[2] highlights the way it works. Have a quick scan of these two people and answer: Who do you prefer, John or Mark?

- John is intelligent, industrious, impulsive, critical, stubborn and jealous.
- Mark is jealous, stubborn, critical, impulsive, industrious and intelligent.

Most people will say John, even though the two descriptions are identical apart from the order of the words. Because people are busy, or lazy, or because of our ancestral need to process information and make rapid decisions, we look at the first part of the description and start to make an assessment which we are reluctant to change later on.

Grasping an understanding of this, it becomes fairly obvious that by simply planning the order in which we offer information, we can change the way in which it is perceived. This form of information management can maximise or damage the way a proposal is viewed. Let's hypothesise how we might apply this to a fictional sports utility vehicle (SUV):

- SUV1 – prestigious, spacious, comfortable, fun, off-road capable, poor road holding, high running costs, hard to park and bad for the environment
- SUV2 – bad for the environment, hard to park, high running costs, poor road holding, off-road capable, fun, comfortable, spacious and prestigious

Although the lists are identical, it's clear which is the most appealing.

Here's another example of priming bias, this time from Daniel Kahneman:[3]

A bat and ball cost $1.10.

The bat costs one dollar more than the ball.

How much does the ball cost?

What do you think?

The answer most people give is $0.10 (or 10 cents).

The actual answer is $0.05 (or 5 cents).

There are two ways of answering this question. One is instinctive and the other is to take time to think carefully. The instinctive approach is heavily influenced by priming – it's hard for the brain to not see $1.10 and the $1 and work out the difference is 10 cents, and then jump to the wrong answer.

Another way to prove the answer is to use algebra. We can work through it together. The mathematics say baseball and bat cost $1.10 together

so **Baseball + Bat = $1.10**   let's call this (a)

and

the bat costs $1.00 more than the baseball

so **Bat = Baseball + $1**   let's call this (b)

Substituting **Bat** in (a) with (b) (**Baseball + $1**). . .

Baseball + Bat = $1.10

(Baseball + $1)

will give us

Baseball + Baseball + $1 = $1.10

or

2 Baseball = $0.10

which means

Baseball = $0.05

So, a baseball is actually $0.05 (or 5 cents), not the 10 cents that our brain often wants to jump to.

Here's another example from Daniel Kahneman. It's best done with a flash card, but try and take a look.

Guess, or roughly estimate, the answers to these two calculations in under 5 seconds

- $1 \times 2 \times 3 \times 4 \times 5 \times 6 \times 7 \times 8 = ?$
- $8 \times 7 \times 6 \times 5 \times 4 \times 3 \times 2 \times 1 = ?$

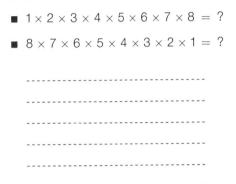

Those with a mathematical slant will realise that the answer for both is identical. However, when this exercise was shown to groups of students the average guesses were very different:

- $1 \times 2 \times 3 \times 4 \times 5 \times 6 \times 7 \times 8 = ?$ Average guess = 512
- $8 \times 7 \times 6 \times 5 \times 4 \times 3 \times 2 \times 1 = ?$ Average guess = 2,250

Again, having the larger numbers first makes the difference.

So, we can see here how powerful priming is, and how open everyone is to its influence. The key question for you to think about is: how can you use priming in your business to improve the way that information, and in particular pricing, is viewed and perceived?

DECREASING SENSITIVITY BIAS

I mentioned that most consumers see themselves as being rational decision makers. However, there are many cases when this can be seen to be incorrect. Decreasing sensitivity bias shows that decisions with equal value are treated very differently if the context changes.

For example, someone is much less likely to be bothered to walk 10 min to save $10 on something costing $600 than they are to do the same 10 min walk to save $10 on a $25 item. The $10 is the same in both cases, as is the effort to save it. So, the attractiveness of the $10 compared to the effort required to save it should be the same. However, despite this logic, the *proportion* that the $10 represents of the overall amount tends to change how valuable It is perceived to be. This is clearly irrational, since $10 is $10 and the amount of effort to save it is the same.

LOSS AVERSION

Loss aversion is a well-known bias where we treat losses differently to perceived gains. In general, losses are felt more keenly than gains.

The idea of loss aversion was introduced in a paper in 1979 by psychologists Daniel Kahneman and Amos Tversky.[4] Kahneman went on to research the cognitive processes used in making economic decisions which led him to winning the 2002 Nobel Prize in economics.

As an example, let's look at this famous case from social sciences, called the 'disease problem':[5]

Imagine there is about to be a disease outbreak and you have to choose between two alternative programmes to tackle the disease for 600 people.

- If you had to choose, which of the following two programmes would you choose?

    A: Certain saving of 200 people

    B: One-third probability that 600 people will be saved, and a two-thirds probability that no people will be saved

Now answer the next alternative question:

- If you had to choose, which of the following two programs would you choose?

    C: Certain death of 400 people

    D: One-third chance that nobody will die, two-thirds chance that 600 people will die

    ----

Most people (72% of participants in the original sample) choose A for the first question and D (78%) for the second question. However, A and C are actually the same, and B and D are the same. When most people choose A and then D they are changing their choice because of the way that the (identical) outcome is phrased. This is because people are far less comfortable with losing something than they are with gaining something. The idea that choices B and C guarantee a loss, articulates this bias, leading them to their choice.

Similarly, if an investment opportunity offers a 50% chance of tripling the invested money but a 50% chance of losing all the money, most people would be reluctant to make the investment. This is because the potential loss is more painful than the value of the gain, despite the fact that, on average, this would be a winning strategy.[6]

It has been noted that investors are more likely to hold on to losing shares and sell winning shares, when in fact the opposite would be more rational.

Business examples of loss aversion include the use of free samples and free initial trial periods such as with free initial subscriptions. Once people have something, the emotional cost of losing it is higher than the cost to retain it. Companies sometimes frame the expiry of a trial subscription as a potential loss in order to articulate the loss aversion bias in the customer.

SOURCE BIAS

Source bias is that which attributes different values to the same thing if the context changes. An example of this can be as easy as the price of a can of Coke. The price that people are willing to pay for a can of Coke in a supermarket store is far less than the price they are willing to pay for the same can of Coke from a shop in a luxury hotel lobby. The can of coke is the same, but the price can be very different.

In a sense, the setting within which the product is being sold is being bundled as part of the offering. However, a rational brain would diagnose this as an identical product being sold at vastly different prices. In the above scenario, visiting a nearby supermarket and bringing back a can of Coke to the hotel would be the rational thing to do.

ANCHORING BIAS

Anchoring is a powerful concept that is used to great effect in many businesses. Let's take an example from the theory of negotiations. We'll recall the example from Chapter 2, buying a rug in a market. This is a typical bargaining situation. You see a rug that you are interested in. There is no price tag on the rug. How much is the rug?

You ask the price. The sellers gives a high price, perhaps you reply with a low price. Perhaps you meet somewhere in between and make a purchase, perhaps you don't find a common price and you move on to the next vendor. This is classic bargaining. The price is unknown and the negotiation process is primarily about price discovery.

A classic question is about making the first offer. Do you make the first offer, or do you ask for a price? Whoever makes the first price offer 'anchors' the negotiation.[7]

It's called an anchor because, just like a marine anchor used by ships, once it's in place it's difficult to move – it's difficult to drag to a new position.

In anchoring, people tend to use the first piece of information they receive to direct their subsequent decisions or actions.

An example of everyday anchoring is the use of price labels in shops. By putting a price on an item, the shop is creating an anchor that is difficult to move. N.B. Difficult, but not impossible. I often set my students the personal development challenge of going into a department store and buying something at a negotiated discount (and yes, surprising though it may sound, it certainly can be done very well).

Another way in which anchoring is used is by placing an expensive item next to a cheaper one: it makes the cheaper one look like good value:

£10,000 watch   £30,000 watch   £2,000 watch

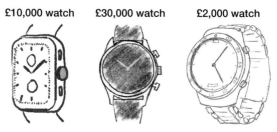

Look at the example above. The use and positioning of the three price points mean that the £2,000 watch begins to look like good value.

Once you are aware of the phenomenon, you can see examples of anchoring all around you.

Framing and priming in reference price points

Shops do this very well – offering a range of prices for similar products. This could be said to be providing products to suit all tastes, but if you look at their most expensive items, ask yourself how often do they really sell those? Or, are they there to make the other items look like spectacularly good value? Layered prices, using multi-price points, is a very powerful technique.

Shops in city centres often display some products with super high prices. Eventually shoppers become recalibrated to high prices, and then the slightly lower price points start to look like good value, or at least good value to the shopper at that particular point in time.

Similarly, there is also what I call the 'emporium effect'. Have you visited an emporium or collection of shops, often all selling a similar product, or products with a common theme? Once you've stepped foot into one of these you've clearly indicated that you are a potential customer, but the emporium effect is one where you see lots of choices, too many choices actually, and that means you need help and advice to choose. Luckily, in the emporium there are many experts willing to advise you on your 'best choice'. Similarly, the multitude of prices means that anchoring takes place. If you were in your home or office environment taking a more rational look at a single price, you'd have a very different view to the view when you've been exposed to a multitude of high prices. Just like the watch example above, when faced with the outrageously expensive, the merely expensive starts to look like good value.

As an aside, it's also worth noting that emporiums can be excellent – hard to beat in fact – if you wish to review many buying options very quickly and, particularly, if you wish to educate yourself on the breadth and variety of options available, which might otherwise be difficult or time consuming to do. This may go some way to explain their enduring popularity.

TACTICAL PRICE POINTS – USING PRICE POINTS AS A ROAD SIGN

Most people would recognise the three price options below from the usual coffee house chains.

Small	Medium	Large
$1.85	$2.10	$2.45

These prices happen to be based on Starbucks' USA coffee prices for a basic cup of coffee, although the relationship holds true for most coffee providers.[8]

So, if you want a coffee, you go into your local coffee shop and you see you can get a cup of coffee for $1.85. However, as your eye scans the row something interesting happens. You realise that for just another 25 cents you can have a much larger coffee, one the size of a 'bucket'. And for another 35 cents after that you can again have an even larger coffee, one the size of a 'bathtub'! They are much better value for money you think. Which should you choose?

Apparently, most people choose *Medium*: according to NATSO,[9] Medium remains the most ordered coffee size by almost a two-to-one margin.

Given the dominance of Medium, why does Small exist? The reason, of course, is that the Small size here is directing you to buy the Medium (or Large). Similar to priming, because Small comes first in the list, it's used as a gauge to assess the options that follow. In other words, the $1.85 is an anchor that directs you to trade up. This is an example of using *tactical price points* to help customers make certain decisions.

On a side note, it's also interesting to see the language in use. Rather than use the word small, some vendors use specialised language – Starbucks calls their 'Small' *Tall*. Whilst 'Medium' is *Grande* and 'Large' is *Venti*.

Let's look at another example. *The Economist* is a well-regarded business magazine that's been around since 1843. According to Dan Ariely of MIT,[10] *The Economist* had the following pricing plan available online

- Web-only subscription $59
- Print-only subscription $125
- Web + print subscription $125

Looking at the choices, you can see it appears that the middle choice is somewhat irrational and redundant. Why would you choose the Print-only subscription when you can have Web + print for the same price?

Dan Ariely then ran a couple of experiments with his audience at MIT, asking them which of the three choices they would choose.

He received the following results:

- Web only subscription $59   16% chose it
- Print only subscription $125   0% chose it
- Web + print subscription $125   84% chose it

This translates into an average spend per customer (or average price) of $114.

This is perhaps what we might expect to see, with the redundant middle choice scoring zero and people choosing either the first or third option.

He then removed the apparently irrational middle option, 'Print only subscription', and ran another experiment. The results are shown below:

- Web only subscription $59   68% chose it
- Web + print subscription $125   32% chose it

This translates into an average spend per customer (or average price) of just $80.

What you can see is a large drop in the number of people choosing 'Web + print subscription' and a large increase in people choosing 'Web-only subscription'. This translates into a huge reduction of 30% in the average price paid. We know how big an influence a mere 1% change of price makes to profitability from Chapter 5, imagine the negative effects of a 30% reduction in average price to the business.

So, what is happening here? Clearly the middle option helped people make their decision, and in a way that benefits *The Economist* (and some would argue, benefits the customer too, since they get to read the magazine). This is another example of tactical price points changing people's decision making.

Interestingly, if we play the above two scenarios in reverse order, we can see an example of how changing the number and spacing of price points can influence average transaction values. Companies use this opportunity to explore this effect within their own pricing strategies. It's true for B2C, but probably also has a tangible effect in B2B too. By introducing or changing the order and number of price points, different average transaction values will be produced. Simple trials should uncover potential improvements.

If you are planning to do this, it's worth considering that, although we can sometimes make informed guesses as to what influences customer decisions in this way, there's no substitute for experimentation to find out what works. Designing and trialling a safe experiment with customers is probably the most reliable method of predicting what will happen as a result of changes you might make.

EMBRACING BIASES

Although most of us believe we are rational, and therefore most other people must be rational too, most of the considerable research evidence is to the contrary. This means that companies that embrace the existence and use of biases discover new ways of either influencing customer behaviour and achieving 'trade-ups', or simply making it easier for the customer to buy.

This is seen everywhere in today's economy, from luxury watches to high-street coffee chains. Given how we've seen that people and markets are often irrational, framing and priming are popular choices by companies to increase value, and often price. More specifically, framing and priming are used by companies to direct customers to the products they should buy, and to direct them to a higher price (which *they* might perhaps argue, is better both for the company and the customer in the long run).

For the informed customer, understanding these biases can, of course, help them avoid being subject to these forms of influence and from making decisions in these ways.

EXERCISE

Identify biases in your own organisation

For your own company, think about how biases may be present in the ways that you make decisions. Are there places where priming overly affects the way that you make decisions? Do you review decisions and the external reference points that you use to frame decisions? Is there a way to ensure you are taking a whole-picture approach?

	Today	This week
Priming bias: First information changes the way subsequent information is perceived.		
Decreasing sensitivity bias: Look for rationality and use numbers to measure things objectively.		
Loss aversion: We treat perceived losses differently to perceived gains. To check, what happens if you rewrite every loss as a gain?		
Source bias: Attributes different values to the same thing if the context changes.		
Anchoring bias: Anchors are difficult to drag to a new position, just like a ship's anchor.		

Guidance: Biases affect people's ability to make rational decisions. This doesn't mean that the wrong decision is always made, but that the process used is not based on rational logic. This exercise is therefore about seeking and increasing rationality – a good practice to develop as it is likely to be far more reliable in the longer run. For each bias, think about whether this bias may be present in your company's processes, procedures and decision making. Consider what influences the way decisions are made. Consider areas where this may be applicable today and also in the next week. Once you've populated the list you can consider whether to challenge the thinking behind specific decisions, what facts they are based upon and whether changes need to be brought about.

CHAPTER SUMMARY

- Research shows that people and markets are frequently highly irrational, despite what they might think or say.

- Cognitive biases such as framing and priming are used by companies as powerful means of increasing value – and thereby price.

- These biases are also often used by companies tactically to direct customers to products whose higher prices will be associated with higher value.

Things to consider

Embracing biases
What customer biases are you aware of?
In what way do competitors use biases to add or remove customer value?

Chapter exercise

Identify biases in your own organisation

CHAPTER 11

OTHER STRATEGIES COMPANIES USE FOR PRICE INCREASES

To reiterate my comments from Chapter 1, when I talk about raising prices in this book I'm not talking about profiteering. Instead, what I have meant by suggesting the raising of prices throughout is finding ways to help high-growth companies to survive and thrive: reinvesting more into product development and staff; making better products; and giving customers more value. In other words, climbing up the value ladder.

There is a clear virtuous cycle here, but many companies attempt to do the second part without a pricing and margin structure to support it sufficiently. After all, business success over the long term is safest when based on developing sustainable competitive advantages and effective business strategies. These often require investments, and investments are easiest to fund from gross and operating profit margins.

Higher prices and margins, leading to more investment in employee training and paying higher salaries, in turn helps to produce a happier, more productive and more skilled workforce.

For both SMEs and start-ups, in particular, finding a way to climb up the value ladder of their sector is a journey to gain access to more prosperous and discerning clients, and establishing suitable prices (in most cases, higher than their current prices) is an important part of this journey.

This chapter therefore develops this theme, going on to review some additional techniques in use by companies today to raise prices. As a consumer, you can also ask yourself to what extent you are subject to these and what you can do about it.

DO THE TWO DOUBLING EXERCISES. CAN YOU DOUBLE YOUR PRICE?

It's sad when I hear of a company or entrepreneur that has gone bust. Very occasionally, I get to speak to the customers of these failed companies, and they sometimes say to me they couldn't believe how cheap the product or service was. What a shame they hadn't shared this information with the company in question! It might have meant their staying in business and avoiding depriving their customers of their service.

I was speaking to a group of partners in a successful London professional services business who were bemoaning the 'closure' of a Swiss watch repair specialist. The specialist had apparently been highly capable of repairing all types of mechanical Swiss watches and was 'unbelievably cheap' compared to High Street shops or to sending the watch to the brand owner, charging instead perhaps a quarter of the comparative price. What a shame they hadn't been more candid with this individual – even a modest rise in price could have meant securing the ongoing availability of the service.

Similarly, I routinely tell my favourite restaurants if I think they are too cheap. If I enjoy the food, I don't wish for them to fail and then be denied their wonderful cuisine. This is most often the case with restaurants that are new start-ups (failure rates of new restaurants are appalling[1]). Often a new restaurant will open, perhaps supporting the aspirational dream of its founder, then after a few months the accounts are compiled and it finds it's highly unprofitable, or things have already run their course, and even before any financial reporting, the business goes into a cash crunch and an overdrawn bank account, shortly followed by closure.

Failure following an unrealistically low sales price is common. A company that could sell at £300 and succeed, instead sells at £100 (for the reasons explained in this book) and goes bust. It may sound like an extreme example, but its offering is lost, depriving customers of choice and reducing competition.

Therefore, think about the price doubling exercises outlined in Chapter 9. Is there a safe way that you can conduct a market test with a price double its current level? If so, I would urge you to design and execute one of the various forms of this test. It almost always yields interesting results, and done correctly it can transform a business. There's also the alternative 'lite' version – perhaps you can do the thought experiment. What would you need to do to justify a doubling of your price? What values, messaging or other aspects would be required to achieve this? The answer to the question may offer insights as to how to progressively increase prices.

OTHER STRATEGIES FOR PRICE INCREASES

An examination of the rationale, potential cognitive roadblocks and approaches to doubling prices has been detailed in this book. However, it's worth highlighting some of the general strategies that companies today use to achieve pricing objectives, not least to familiarise ourselves enough to avoid being engaged in these ways.

COVERT OR OVERT?

Broadly speaking, companies use two different ways to increase prices, they use overt means and they use covert means.

Overt means are of course transparent and visible. For example, an overt way of increasing price is to simply double the *sticker price.*

By contrast, covert means of raising prices are less obvious or are hidden, sometimes obfuscating the price, or requiring the customer to do extra work to find the real price. A covert method usually leaves the sticker price unchanged, or undefined, but increases the size of the value of the average transaction. We saw in Chapter 2 that transaction value is an important way that companies effectively increase price overall. The financial services industry has sometimes done this, hiding fees and not showing the real price, and sometimes this has attracted the attention of the industry regulator.[2]

Both approaches have pros and cons and we'll look at many examples in this chapter. It's worth noting that it's not necessarily an either/or choice of one approach or the other. Some companies use both approaches simultaneously. Personally, I advocate transparency and honesty in all business dealings; making the price clear to customers and using overt means of increasing transaction sizes are almost always ethically superior practices.

INCREASED DIFFERENTIATION AND THE ROLE OF BRAND

Companies have realised that the less able customers are to make price comparisons, the easier it is to have a price which is independently anchored from competitors. Therefore, one of the ways to make it harder for comparisons is to increase differentiation, or to increase how different an offering is seen compared to competitors.

Earlier, I mentioned the idea of the USP – as a reminder, this is the thing the company does, which customers value, and is in some way different (and better) than the competition. The elements of the USP are an important means that you can use to communicate to customers why they should buy. Therefore, a good question to ask yourself is: How can you make your USP clearer in the mind of the customer? How to make it usefully unique, more special?

I talked about branding and injecting emotional value in Chapter 6, and emotional value is a key aspect of products and services in today's sophisticated markets. The company brand, and the associated messaging that goes with the brand are key to communicate this value, and thereby change how customers perceive the offering. When I say 'brand' I do not mean just the physical logo of a company, but I mean the combination of the company name, its visual imagery and, most importantly, the messages and values that are associated with it and are being used or reflected in and by its communications.

In fact, a marketer I met who worked for a fast-moving consumer goods (FMCG) company claimed that the valuation of any company beyond the net value of its balance sheet is due to the value of the brand. In other words, the brand itself produces the premium over the net asset value. By contrast, the more traditional view would be that the value of a company is determined by how profitable it is, or perhaps how cash generative it is over time. The idea of a non-tangible asset such as a brand dominating valuation may be a marketer's view, but it's an interesting one nonetheless.

According to *Forbes,* some of the top 15 most valuable brands in the world include Coca-Cola, Apple, Louis Vuitton and Toyota (see Table 11.1).[3] I've chosen to highlight these four because in reading their names you probably already have a view of what the company and its products stand for, what its values are. Also, this message varies by who the audience is, since all of these companies are both B2B and B2C (or, indeed, B2B2C). So, a B2B customer of Amazon Web Service may think of technical capability and reliability, whilst a consumer may think of service excellence and wide variety of choice. Rather than just tangible value, all of these aspects have a healthy amount of emotional value.

If we look at Louis Vuitton from a consumer perspective, what are the values and messages associated with that brand? As with all luxury goods brands, the benefits are largely intangible and associated with how they make the consumer feel. People generally buy luxury goods because doing so makes them feel better: better about themselves, the world and perhaps the future. This intangible aspect directs them to purchase a luxury product at prices as much as ten times higher than ones with similar functionality

Table 11.1 Forbes' annual list of the world's most valuable brands, $billion

Rank	Brand	Brand value	Brand revenue	Industry
1	Apple	$241.2	$260.2	Technology
2	Google	$207.5	$145.6	Technology
3	Microsoft	$162.9	$125.8	Technology
4	Amazon	$135.4	$260.5	Technology
5	Facebook	$70.3	$49.7	Technology
6	Coca-Cola	$64.4	$25.2	Beverages
7	Disney	$61.3	$38.7	Leisure
8	Samsung	$50.4	$209.5	Technology
9	Louis Vuitton	$47.2	$15	Luxury
10	McDonald's	$46.1	$100.2	Restaurants

(see Chapter 4 to remind yourself of some similar examples). Such is the power of emotional content.

Understanding what values customers have is one of the key steps to introducing emotional content to the offering of a high-growth business. If we can understand the values that our customers have then we can find ways to connect or link to them. Introducing emotional value is not normally therefore an introspective exercise – usually, we have to 'get out of the building' and interact with customers. What's useful is to get under the skin of the customer. By understanding our customers in this way, we can design our brand, our messaging and our strategy in ways that address and support their values, and in a way usefully different to our competitors – thereby increasing our differentiation.

A simple example of this was when I was approached by a partner from an accountancy company that wished to grow. It was a relatively small, but nonetheless successful, firm based in a provincial city in the UK. The partner wanted to know how to accomplish growth and gain new clients in a market that wasn't growing particularly fast. I asked what it was that they said to win over new customers in a sales conversation. The partner answered, 'We explain to the potential customer that we are a professionally qualified firm, that we are diligent, honest and charge a fair price.' I had to point out the rather obvious, that these were all points of parity. Any plausible accountancy practice was likely to be able to make identical claims.

Many businesses do not truly differentiate themselves from their competition. Instead, they essentially have virtually identical offerings that do not broadcast sufficiently clear messages of why choose them. Many businesses make identical claims to each other, and in competitive situations these points of parity do little to encourage the hesitating potential customer to buy or switch, unless they happen to be unhappy with their current provider. This can be particularly important if the market is not growing, if new customers are not being created, meaning that every new sale is at the expense of a competitor.

Going back to the accountancy example, instead of proffering points of parity what was needed were points of difference, or some differentiation: What made this firm special? What would really make a client give them their business rather than giving it to another firm? Even if they could not genuinely claim better customer services, higher customer satisfaction rates, faster response times to queries or any other competitive advantages, a notion of uniqueness was required.

There are always opportunities to be more creative, particularly if it's genuinely difficult to find obvious points of difference. A quick 'thought experiment' can offer hints on how to create differentiation and highlight this principle: given the accounting practice was city based and most cities have some social issues of one kind or another, they could perhaps align themselves with, or even start, a local charity which addresses some of the problems in the city. Therefore, when making a future customer sales call, they could, instead of their previous pitch, talk about their charitable work, all of their accomplishments, that they were trying to alleviate some of the societal problems faced within that city, for the benefit of the whole community. By the time that they finish speaking about this, perhaps the potential clients wouldn't be asking them whether they were professionally qualified, or diligent, but would instead be much more likely to look upon them as a favourable partner and as a firm worthy of support. This example is purely a thought experiment (it would need validation before proceeding), but the key point is the finding of ways to differentiate yourself, that make you distinct, and if you can do this in a manner that aligns with your customers' values then it can be a very successful strategy.

On this theme of points of parity, have you ever been to a restaurant that says their chefs are not terribly well qualified, that they hire the cheapest waiting staff, and they extensively use frozen produce? Of course not. Instead, every restaurant says that it has fabulous chefs, they use the freshest produce and have highly skilled chefs producing tasty high-quality food. These again are points of parity, and if every restaurant is making exactly the same claim, then there is no differentiation to help customers choose. The more successful restaurants find ways to differentiate themselves in their offering (including messaging) that provides customer value.

The challenge therefore for any entrepreneur is to differentiate themselves in a useful manner that somehow creates emotional value for customers through this combination of messaging and values (and for restaurants, in addition to providing good food!).

REAL PRICE CAN BE DIFFERENT TO STATED PRICE

Some industries obfuscate the real prices that customers will pay. A well-known example is the discount airline industry, who may advertise a flight at £1, but that price is not what the customer pays. The customer also has to pay taxes, they have to pay extra if they wish to check luggage into the hold, for a meal onboard, for early boarding, for a choice of seats, and, until recently, to actually pay for the flight they needed to pay a fixed and high surcharge to use any reasonable form of card payment (this last practice has been targeted by legislators and is now far less common). Furthermore, once 'captured' on board the aircraft, the customer will be assaulted by various on-sells such as lottery cards, food and drink offers, destination city transport tickets and so on.

Online marketplaces also employ similar techniques of hiding the real prices. Whereas services such as Amazon Prime show a price which is inclusive of a premium delivery service, other sellers through Amazon marketplaces or vendors such as eBay often split the price from the shipping cost. Many online search engines, including those which are embedded within the apps and websites of many of these providers, will look for a best deal based on the stated price despite this often not including the shipping cost. This means that whilst one provider offers a price of £100 including shipping another might post a price of £30 plus shipping costs of £200. The shipping cost is clearly being used tactically. The low 'price' gets a superior result in the search rankings and a careless consumer may miss the shipping costs until much later in the purchase process, or altogether.

This approach 'games' the customer search process and is not laudable, but clearly it must work to some extent because it can be found being widely used. At the time of writing, eBay does allow product search results to be listed by lowest price *including* postage ('lowest price + P&P'), whilst Amazon only offers results to be ranked by price without postage. However, in the spirit of enterprise, eBay sellers have found a way to get around the 'lowest price + P&P' sorting feature by including lower-priced goods within the same listing as an option. So, something costing £10 is listed along with a £1 cable as an either/or option of the same product, and the search algorithm uses the lower figure and displays the £10 item at the £1 position.

OFFER OPTIONS: USE PRICING MENUS

Often, a high-growth business won't know how much the customer wishes to spend. It won't know how much budget is available, the risk being that the price could have been higher, and a lower quoted price will 'leave money on the table'. A technique companies use to get around this is to allow the customer to guide them as to how much they wish to spend by using pricing menus and extensions. This is one specific way of implementing on-sells or upsells.

A good example of this is the car industry. If I look at the website for the Range Rover, I can buy a standard-trim long-base vehicle for £115,960. This therefore is a fairly premium price point for a car. However, there are many different variants available at many different price points. This 'spread' of offers is a good example of a pricing menu allowing customers to express their appetite for the product through the different price points.

Furthermore, if we tick all the option boxes on the Range Rover car builder website, the total we can spend on a Range Rover comes to a grand total of £211,454. That's a difference of £95,494, or a potential 82% increase over the base model. This means that customers who have more to spend are invited to increase their transaction size by up to 82%. Only Range Rover will know what the variable costs associated with fitting those options are, and the contribution to profits thereby produced, but this pricing menu is a good illustration of raising price by increasing average transaction size.

Similarly, companies often consider ways in which they can encourage their customers to indicate their willingness to seek a more premium offering through 'power ups' or a menu of options. This is particularly useful when a company is unsure of what the actual budget is. If customers have extra budget available, they can make use of it, as long as they are given valuable reasons to do so.

ON-SELLING AND UPSELLING THE CUSTOMER

Once companies have acquired a customer, having gone to the expense and effort of essentially recruiting a customer who is in a position to buy from them, it's a shame not to maximise that opportunity. Here are two techniques used by companies which are very useful ways of increasing the total customer spend.

On-selling is the technique of offering additional products to be added to the 'basket' that the customer purchases in the transaction.

By contrast, *upselling* offers the customer the opportunity to increase the size or quantity of the product that they're buying in the transaction.

These two techniques are incremental, in that they operate from an already established position, which is then enhanced.

Pertinent everyday examples of these two techniques can be found in the restaurant and hospitality industry. Fast food restaurants are good at upselling – asking customers if they would like to increase the size of, or 'supersize', their meal (and, somewhat notoriously, supersize their waistbands!). Similarly, staff in coffee shops are often trained to say 'Would you like medium or large?' when asked by a customer for a coffee or other product without specifying what size they would like – in doing so, the staff member is not offering the small size. The verbal offer perhaps implies to the customer that these are the most popular choices, so there's an element of giving advice to the customer, or of adopting social norms. Perhaps the customer has already been primed to ignore the 'poor value' small-sized option, as we saw in Chapter 10. Or, it's simply a way to remove the lower-priced option from immediate consideration.

Restaurants are also good at on-selling, so in a more formal restaurant the waiting staff taking the order will often make suggestions for additional side dishes, or additional plates that the customers might particularly enjoy ('Some olives to share perhaps?' or 'Some bread and dips?') – therefore increasing the number of items that are being purchased, which increases the total transaction size in terms of value.

Applied well, and with good ethical practices in place, these two techniques should be transparent and fair. However, some companies aren't so clear. Many times, in a restaurant the waiter will offer an upsell or on-sell but not give a price. Similarly, 'a special of the day' is sometime described at the table without a price being mentioned – it's most unusual that the special of the day in this setting is at a low price point. The menu of course has prices for regular items, but this verbal delivery often omits them. Many a customer is surprised at the high cost of the special or option that they unwittingly agreed to. These add-ons or premium offerings executed correctly increase the average transaction size, increasing the effective price through the framework we looked at in Chapter 5.

MODIFY DAY RATES VS TOTALS

Many service industries work by charging a day rate for services and then quoting a number of days required to carry out a piece of work. By multiplying the two together, an overall price is arrived at.

However, companies have found that it's important to avoid customer 'hot buttons' – which is to say, things which 'ring alarm bells' for a customer, or things which are very easy to compare – and a high day rate can sometime be such a button. Some companies get around such issues by reducing the day rate, but then increasing the number of days in the knowledge, or expectation, that it will increase the probability of success. This, of course, mispresents the actual time being spent on a piece of work for a client, but is a way to make the supplier look less expensive and the work look more laborious than it is. (To try and give a balanced view, I should point out that the staff in many of these companies work well beyond an eight-hour working day, so the notion of a 'day rate' is already somewhat enfeebled.)

Just like the cognitive biases explored in Chapters 2 and 10, busy customers look for *shortcuts* to make decisions. Finding out what the 'hot buttons' are for customers and avoiding them can be important for high-growth businesses.

USE BUNDLING

Bundling is where a product or service is sold along with other products or services. They are therefore sold together as one sale unit. When they are sold together in this way, usually there's a single price for the whole bundle. Bundling is often positioned as a better value proposition for customers, and this may be the case, but it also has an important role for companies in raising transaction value.

Bundling produces an increase in transaction value, and therefore effective price, in at least two ways.

First, it can make it more difficult for the customer to discover the separate prices for the individual elements, therefore preventing price shopping comparisons with competitors. This is particularly true if the elements are not available for sale (and thereby priced individually) outside of the bundle.

Second, by persuading the customer to buy the extra elements in the bundle, that they may not have otherwise purchased, the overall spend goes up. Usually, the bundle price is positioned lower than the prices of the individual elements added together, and this makes the bundle good value in both appearance and reality.

Bundles are very common. Bundles are similar in a way to on-selling, but rather than being incremental to an established position at the time of the sell, a bundle is usually a starting point for a transaction.

Everyday examples of bundles include meal deals in fast food restaurants, and software such as Microsoft Office. Meal deal bundles are often a sandwich, a drink and a snack. This 'deal' is cheaper than the individual elements added together, and many people purchase them, even if they would not normally have chosen the exact same size and element combinations if the meal deal didn't exist. The overall transaction size is thereby increased.

Software is often bundled in a similar way. Microsoft Office includes a word processor (Word), a spreadsheet (Excel), a presentation program (PowerPoint) and other programs. These can include between three and twelve individual pieces of software in a variety of bundles. Microsoft also offers a choice of an annual fee, or an outright purchase,[4] for either one user, or a specified group of users. Originally, a word processor such as Word or a spreadsheet such as Excel was available for individual purchase, but I couldn't find availability of the individual elements to purchase today. Customers just purchase the bundle, even if they do not want or will not use all of the elements.

A book publisher might bundle a series of books into a box set. Customers might be tempted to buy the set for completeness rather than the titles they strictly want.

Amazon Prime bundles delivery, music, video and much more. Mobile telephony companies bundle minutes, data and texts. Landline companies bundle telephony, Internet, and video. Restaurants bundle their dishes via set menus.

Bundles can include disparate elements, so products can be bundled with warranties or service plans. Services or products can be bundled with training, or maintenance plans and so on. Cars are similarly often sold with warranties and service plans included in the price – an on-sell might be a finance deal, and often this has a better margin associated with it than the actual physical car.

In many of these cases, the bundles are actually more popular than the purchasing of individual items. If this is the case, and if this is the intended strategy, then companies use the price points of the individual items as a signal to direct customers to purchase the bundle, i.e. the individual prices are largely there to underline how great a deal the bundle is. This is another example of how companies can set reference prices to direct buyer behaviour.

How exactly you can use bundling in your business depends on the specifics, as ever, but bundling is a powerful feature in many industries.

ESTABLISH MULTIPLE PRICE POINTS

Many companies will sell multiple products at different price points. These might include different versions or varieties of the same product, or similar products. For example, some may have different features, some may be more premium in terms of what they offer, some may be more basic.

From a customer perspective this offers the opportunity to choose the option that is most suited to their needs. Without this simple facility, with a single offering, there would be an element of guesswork of whether it was particularly suitable to any customer. In other words, the variety gives the customer the benefit of making the best decision, of finding the best fit. This principle of getting customers to indicate to you their preferences is an important one.

Of course, the degree to which the different related products vary in terms of their features and benefits, as well as their price, is up to the company providing them. Companies have found it's quite possible to use a strategic approach of modifying and changing the differences in product characteristics and price in order to find which combination works best in terms of business success.

Again, you can consider what actual differences in product characteristics is required for your company. They may be very large such as the difference between a budget and top-end smartphone, or they may be more nuanced and simply based on branding and values, such as we found with the water products in Chapter 4. Even where the products are physically identical, we have seen that they can be differentiated in terms of value and the messages they communicate.

AIRLINES AND FIRST CLASS

As an everyday example, let's think about the passenger airline business. In the pre-jet age, air travel was expensive and restricted to those who could afford to pay the very high prices required. The service levels were also typically high, as might be expected by customers able to afford the premium price points. The introduction of the gas turbine heralded the jet age, and dramatically lower travelling costs became available for the first time. This led in turn to lower prices. However, the industry noticed that there remained the appetite for higher price points. Therefore, first class and then business class travel were developed as alternative options. The primary advantage of modern air travel is the vastly reduced travel times compared to alternatives. However, a strictly rational view might note that all passengers arrive at the final destination at the same time, despite some paying ten times as much for essentially the same journey.

ADOPTING DIFFERENT PRICING FOR DIFFERENT CLASSES OF CLIENTS

As mentioned in Chapter 9, some companies have products or services that can serve several different sectors. In one sector the going market rate, or price, for a solution can be very different to another. By segmenting clients according to the pricing norms in their particular industry, companies have found that it's possible to tailor different price points to different situations. High-growth companies that do this find it both increases the chances of the proposition being well received, and supports higher margins in those sectors with higher price expectations.

USE PRICING RUNWAYS

Earlier, I mentioned the problem of not knowing how much a potential customer is able, willing, or wishes to pay. One technique companies use to solve this problem is the pricing runway approach. It's another method that some companies use to establish the available budget of the customer and some calibration to the level competitors are quoting. This technique is used where customer relationships, once established, are likely to continue and is in contrast to supply agreements which go through a formal review such as competitive tendering. It also tends to take place when the transaction size of the purchase is not very large nor material for the customer.

The way in which companies use this technique is that a new customer relationship is established at a relatively low price, with the price tag rising over time. This is similar to an aircraft taking off on a runway – it starts at ground level, then once it's picked up speed, starts to rise into the air. As an example, many subscription-based B2B offerings work this way. Prices start at a level likely to create a purchase decision, then they increase over time. In some cases, the price rises are the same for all customers, but in the most sophisticated cases, each individual client can be on its own stage on the pricing runway, or on a parallel runway altogether, with prices they pay being different to other clients for the same offering. There are examples of pricing runways in professional membership industries where the cost or effort of switching to a new provider is high, but also in cable and satellite TV industries where those who are reluctant to pay the increases eventually negotiate their own rate, with many consumers paying different prices for the same package according to their propensity for price acceptance.

This strategy is often used by companies when the clients are 'sticky'. 'Sticky' simply means that once a client has been acquired, they are unlikely to revisit their purchase decision without a strong external stimulus. Therefore, companies using runways ask themselves how sticky their clients are. 'Stickiness' can be caused by high switching costs (the requirement for an unappealing amount of work, or effort, or money for making a new purchase) or a low-priority classification for the product (it's an immaterial issue, or seen as low value, lost in the background 'noise' of issues).

A classic example of stickiness in the UK is the checking, or current, bank account. The statistics have long proven that people in the UK are more likely to get divorced than change their bank.[5]

Companies have found that if their strategic success is based on stickiness/retention, and they are not at the higher end of the transaction size spectrum, then it would make sense to gently but actively increase prices for repeat accounts – that is, have customers on pricing runways.

USE PRICES ENDING IN .99

There's a well-known phenomenon whereby customers perceive prices to be lower if the price ends with a '.99'. This is particularly true where this reduces the size of the first number. For example:

$**4**.99 is perceived as being much lower than $**5**

$**9**.99 is perceived as much lower than $**10**

$**4**9.99 is much lower than $**5**0.

However, it is far less effective when the first number remains unchanged, so:

$**4**8.99 is not seen as being much lower than $**4**9

$**1**74.99 is not seen as being much lower than $**1**75

This phenomenon is largely due to the priming bias covered in the previous chapter. It's worth noting that this type of pricing becomes problematic when prices have to eventually be raised (for example, due to inflation) and they thereby cross some of these price lines. If the leading digit has to increase, it can then cause perceptions of a much larger price rise.

MANAGING OVER-DEMAND

If there is excess demand for the available amount of product, then companies find there's an opportunity to select the best customers. In the pricing context, the best customers will usually be those premium customers willing to pay a higher price.

Airlines do this by raising prices as a particular flight starts to fill up. The later the seat booked, the higher the price. If an airline followed 'cost plus' pricing this would be illogical because the earlier sales cover the cost of the flight, whist the marginal cost of one more passenger on a nearly full flight is close to zero, so the seats should become cheaper. As we've previously seen, 'cost plus' is often problematic. Clearly, airlines have realised that in this scenario the scarcity of supply overrides such flawed logic.

When I was helping to build one of the early internet companies in 2000, I travelled with a team to Boston to meet with a well-known specialist website builder, who was a leader in this field. We were interested in having a website built, plus having some extra functionality developed such as using the webcam to show the website user's face next to some of the products being sold. The quotation we received from the developer was $190,000 for the website plus another $230,000 for the webcam work.[6] These figures were over ten times higher than we expected. We knew that the supplier was incredibly busy – since the whole world was building or buying websites at that time. They had clearly decided to maximise the value of the remaining capacity in the face of overwhelming demand. They were only willing to squeeze us into their work capacity if we were willing to pay a hefty premium. We declined the offer but I'm sure they found someone else to fill the remaining capacity – at least until the 'dot bomb' market crash which followed the next year.

This website example is perhaps a little extreme, but often companies use escalating prices in a progressive manner as capacity reduces – to both manage overdemand and to reap the rewards of popularity. This maximises profitability of the marginal sale – once capacity reaches zero, no new sales can be made, even if there is extra demand at any price.

GET PREMIUM CUSTOMERS TO SELF-IDENTIFY

In their book *Freakonomics,* authors Stephen J. Dubner and Steven Levitt highlight email scams, usually claiming to be from Nigeria, that were sent to many millions of people.[7] In the scam a poorly worded and largely non-credible email asks for recipients to help 'liberate' a large sum of money from Nigeria. In order to do so, at some point they need to offer their own bank details to the scammer.

The pertinent question that Dubner and Levitt asked is why are the emails so poorly worded and so obviously scams? Why weren't the scammers trying harder to hide their deceit? The answer, they suggest, is that the poor design is actually deliberate, so that anyone who does reply has almost certainly self-identified as being someone gullible and therefore more likely to go ahead with the process. In effect, the poor writing of the email text is designed to help identify easy targets.

Although scam emails and scammers are truly deplorable, the concept of finding ways to get customers to self-identify to your business is a perfectly valid one.

There are many examples of this idea being used. High-end jewellers have intimidating store fronts, often without any prices displayed. This is presumably to deter time wasting economy shoppers from entering, or ringing the bell to be admitted. Those who do enter have identified themselves as 'being in the market', so to speak, for a premium offering. It may also, in some way, commit someone who crosses the threshold to making a purchase or feel they risk losing face.

Similarly, some art galleries and retail stores require customers to make an appointment in order to shop. This again is a clear strategy to get customers to self-identify as being in the premium target group of customers. I similarly described the *emporium effect* in Chapter 10, where customers identify themselves by entering the premises.

In *open banking,* consumers give permission for companies to view their finances and offer them services. In the realm of permission marketing, consumers allow their profiles to be used to generate offers in which they are likely to be interested – this is especially true for online advertising.

REMEMBER TO REVISIT PRICE OFTEN, IF NOT CONTINUOUSLY

In an earlier chapter we saw the big 'lever' that is price, on average giving over 11% more operating profit for a mere 1% change in price – and these increased profits can then be reinvested into improving products and services.

However, once set, most companies do not revisit pricing decisions often enough, sometimes ignoring it for long periods of time, or only taking the time to consider it when they are under pressure to take a decision to pursue a new piece of business.

It seems in these cases that once price is established, the focus shifts to operational matters, and to the day-to-day management of sales leads and promotional activities. One of the problems of only reactively reviewing prices (when they have to) is that there's not normally the time nor the will to make a proper decision based on collecting the appropriate information about competition, the customer's decision-making landscape, nor reviewing what framing, priming and other biases may be present which could negatively influence the decision.

By contrast, organisations that actively manage their price, that actively look for ways to review their pricing decisions dynamically and regularly, can have more favourable outcomes. They are better prepared, have trained themselves to think entrepreneurially about price, and have progressive plans in place to achieve superior transaction values.

So, to help smarter pricing, ask these useful questions: How can you make a proactive plan around price? How often do you reassess your price points? What approach do you take to doing this? What are your points of reference? How much do you understand about what's 'on the table'? What dynamics can you introduce to increase transaction value?

EXERCISE

How will you use the strategies?

For your company, think about how you could or should apply the strategies from this chapter. To help frame the opportunity for each, you can list the enablers (things that support the use of the strategy) and blockers (things that negate its use) to help you judge the appropriateness and potential for each strategy.

1. Do the two doubling exercises
Enablers:
Blockers:
2. Increased differentiation and the role of brand
Enablers:
Blockers:
3. Real price can be different from stated price
Enablers:
Blockers:
4. Offer options: Use pricing menus
Enablers:
Blockers:
5. On-sell and upsell your customer
Enablers:
Blockers:
6. Modify day rates vs totals
Enablers:
Blockers:

7. Use bundling
Enablers:
Blockers:
8. Establish multiple price points
Enablers:
Blockers:
9. Use pricing runways
Enablers:
Blockers:
10. Use prices ending in .99
Enablers:
Blockers:
11. Managing over-demand
Enablers:
Blockers:
12. Get premium customers to self-identify
Enablers:
Blockers:
13. Remember to revisit price often, if not continuously
Enablers:
Blockers:

Guidance: Review how each of the strategies should potentially be used within your own organisation. The use of enablers and blockers is a method to list the 'pros' and 'cons' for each. You can do this by asking yourself: What is the potential for increasing customer value? What are the dynamics at play? What trials or experiments could be used to fill in any information gaps? You could also consider differing timeframes – what might be impossible today might be a strategic imperative tomorrow.

CHAPTER SUMMARY

■ Most companies don't revisit their pricing decisions often enough, some-times for damagingly long periods.

■ This makes little sense when a 1% improvement in price can give four times more 'bang per buck' than a 1% improvement in sales.

■ Companies frequently use both overt and covert means to set and raise prices. Covert means include leaving the headline price unchanged, but uti-lising other elements to increase overall transaction size.

■ Proven strategies companies use for increasing price include

  ■ establishing multiple price points

  ■ increasing differentiation

  ■ use pricing menus

  ■ on-selling/upselling

  ■ avoiding pricing hot buttons

  ■ using bundling

  ■ pricing runways

  ■ using over-demand

  ■ introducing emotional value (and enhanced branding)

  ■ adopting different pricing for different customer classes

  ■ using pricing runways to manage ongoing rises

  ■ getting premium customers to self-identify.

Things to consider

Overt or covert
Do companies in your sector use covert or overt prices increases?

Brand
What role does brand have in adding value in your industry?

Techniques used
Which techniques do companies use in your sector to raise prices? *e.g. differentiation, emotional value, pricing menus, on-selling, upselling, totals, bundling, multi-points, runways, excess demand*

Chapter exercise

How will you use the strategies?

CHAPTER 12

ON THE ROAD TO SUCCESS

n recent years, with the attractiveness and availability of a 'job for life' largely disappearing, there has been a marked rise in interest in entrepreneurship. This has been supported by numerous programmes at schools, colleges, universities and business schools, and by the advent of platforms such as Kickstarter, IndieGoGo, Seedrs and CrowdCube, which help start and fund companies. Various government grants and tax incentives also encourage business ownership. On the whole, it has never been easier – or more tempting – to establish a firm.

For many reasons, not least as innovators and as employers, these high-growth companies should be supported. They need financial assistance, whether from government, lenders, venture capitalists or other sources of capital; and they also need nonfinancial assistance – most notably management expertise – whether from proven entrepreneurs, business advisors, business schools or other sources of know-how.

For larger and long-established businesses, the calling to entrepreneurial thinking is equally strong. Large businesses form an essential part of any nation's ecosystem. Their size enables them to achieve economies of scale which are not available to smaller companies, and their stability offers employment and long-term planning essential to many stakeholders, including investors. Larger businesses are often also a natural destination for the acquisition and then integration of high-growth start-ups – often new and innovative technology companies – offering a final and important link in the process of technology transfer from research to rolling out across the world. As an example, Apple, well known as a technology innovator, has acquired well over 100 early stage companies. These acquisitions were generally of companies that had developed interesting technologies or created innovative market positions[1] in growing premium markets.

Larger businesses, however, also have their challenges. They are said to be much like a super cargo ship: complex, slow to respond and difficult to steer. Their complexity offers a continuing distraction to management from those tasks which are most important to both risk management and also entrepreneurial thinking. Initiatives to improve the quality of decision making by boards of directors, such as the UK's Combined Code of Corporate Governance, highlight the importance of entrepreneurial perspectives.

All of this is, of course, predicated on having a customer value proposition that is positive, and ideally in some way unique or well differentiated from that of competitors. Although we looked at these topics throughout the book, it is worth restating that long-term competitiveness is safest when it is based on sustainable competitive advantages and a compelling strategy – which are usually derived from internally generated innovation of the product or service, and/or a rapid 'sensing' mechanism within the organisation that can quickly spot and execute market opportunities.

Having established all of this, it's worth reviewing our journey and then adding a few new topics to think about, to help achieve these overall aims.

If, through this book, I've helped you to realise even a 1% price improvement for your company, and you can reinvest the 11% increase in profits this typically generates, then I've been successful.

BRINGING IT ALL TOGETHER

N.B. Please see the collated Smart Pricing Summary Workbook section and questions to ask yourself.

At the beginning of this book, I explained that a key intention in writing this book is to help companies make better use of pricing in order to thrive and survive. This includes SMEs, who are often the innovators of the economy, but also large corporations – both are sources of great value to society and economy, not least through paying taxes and offering employment and, as such, they're companies that should be supported through good commercial management know-how.

What is often missing within such organisations is a formal recognition of the importance and influence of pricing and then, to follow, a pricing process and methodology for the organisation to use to ensure it's maximising the potential that smart pricing offers.

Since much of this book has been about ways of recognising and understanding customer value, rather than using the old fashioned and limited cost-based approaches to pricing, an alternative title to this book might have been 'The death of cost-plus pricing'. However, the book title is quite rightly *Double Your Price!* This is an admirably robust challenge, and I hope you now have some new insights on why, when, and how to consider doing this. There has also been a focus on market testing and using customer experiments to overcome complexity and learn more about customer perceptions of value and how this translates into pricing decisions.

Much of this book has also been about reprogramming the business-person's brain and changing approaches to, and understanding the prioritisation of, pricing. Part of this journey was intended to help shed the baggage of cognitive biases and any sense of guilt companies have about pricing. Another part of the journey has been about explaining the importance of actively managing price and highlighting some approaches companies use to help do this.

FINDING THE RIGHT APPROACH FOR THE RIGHT OPPORTUNITY AND RIGHT MARKET

It is therefore my hope that you will have found a few *nuggets of gold* to help you reshape the way you think about price. As I explained earlier, the suggestions and approaches in a book on this topic cannot be 100% complete or omnipotent, because different industries and sectors have very different structures and differing approaches to gaining sales – with diverse dynamics, rules, norms and associated success factors. Nonetheless, I hope that the breadth of approaches and perspectives you have read about give you useful ideas and food for thought.

In this book we've seen how underpricing is the #1 error of innovative businesses. Innovation poses some special challenges due to a lack of exemplars or established norms. Not only small or new businesses, but large corporations also make critical errors on how important setting price is. Instead, the convenient focus for the entrepreneur or the manager tends to be on top-line growth, without enough consideration of the sustainability of operations and the all-important dynamic of generating cash for reinvestment.

In Chapter 2, we heard some of the arguments and justifications that companies make as to why they cannot raise prices, the role of cognitive biases in their management thinking, and how actually, most successful high-growth businesses charge a relatively premium price for their products. The most visual consequence of not charging a high enough price is the lack of money to pay the staff well, but the more serious implication is a perpetual lack of funds to reinvest in product development and to support growing cash flow requirements.

In Chapter 3 we reviewed the relationship between price and value. We saw that it's not only early stage businesses that don't spend enough time on pricing, larger corporations too make the same error. Some examples highlighted that even just a small increase in price, or average transaction value, would have meant reaching break-even for several recent high-profile corporate collapses.

Next, we reviewed traditional pricing theory and how, as consumers, we have been programmed to accept certain rules and concepts, usually without asking about the underlying logic. We saw that many functionally identical products are sold at multiple price points and, actually, some products are routinely sold, and sell well, at price points three times to ten times of the price of their peers – despite being essentially identical. This result alone should excite the entrepreneurially spirited – a 'door opening' to new and sophisticated opportunities for differentiation and success. We also saw that companies (usually) can't be the cheapest and the best and still expect to make money.

In Chapter 5, we defined what growth means in the context of a high growth business and considered research from *Harvard Business Review* that measured the huge influence price has on profits. It highlighted that a change in price has almost four times the magnitude effect on profits than the same change in sales. Research from McKinsey also suggested nonlinear relationships that some companies take advantage of when they actively price – with big differences in the level of scrutiny given to prices by customers across different categories of product.

As we saw with our generic Company A and B example, it's perfectly possible to have a higher price and lose some potential customers, to convert less leads into sales than would be the case with a lower price, and yet still have a much more profitable enterprise. Such an enterprise is more able to reinvest in important strategic areas and therefore grow well. We also looked at working capital, explained why some businesses 'go bust' by increasing their sales rapidly, and the role of pricing to avoid that.

We then moved on to challenge the validity of 'cost-plus' pricing strategies for high-growth businesses. Despite its enduring popularity, 'cost plus' does not meet any of the key demands of a well-differentiated product in a modern economy.

It can also detrimentally shift the focus of the company's offering from their customer's perspective (which is useful) to the introspective one of internal operations (which is far less useful).

As a much better alternative, we looked at how value-based pricing seeks to understand what value actually means to the customer and how to use this information to set price. Within this context of understanding value, we also looked at the significance of customer reference points, bundling products together and the importance of adding emotional value. We also saw some ways in which destructive price competition is avoided by some sectors, whilst simultaneously pulling off the trick of increasing customer-perceived value.

Chapter 7 is one of the most important chapters. It highlights research using brain scans which seems to prove that, all things being equal, many people actually receive more physical reward when they pay more. Previous studies of similar products being sold at vastly different price points had indicated that price has a strong influence on customers' perception of quality and on how they judge the value derived from a product. But the brain scans actually *show* that this counter-intuitive phenomenon is physically represented in the brain. The reward centres in subjects' brains are energised by a high price point irrespective of whether the product is different or not. This important result goes some way to help us reset our own assumptions about our own rationality, that of our customers, as well as our approaches to setting price.

Chapter 8 explained the mechanism by which reinvesting profits back into a high-growth business can generate large financial returns. Often, the internal rate of return of a high-growth company or innovative project is 25% to 50%. Every pound or dollar that can be reinvested will grow at that compound rate each and every year to follow. Comparing this reinvestment dynamic with a company that has lower prices and simply pays out dividends shows the very different outcomes, even after just a few years.

In the next chapter a challenge was set. Can you double your price? Or, more accurately, are there safe tests you can carry out in the market to see what happens if you double your price? The question was also posed, 'What do you need to do to justify this price increase?' Many companies have tried this test and often they find the exercise very rewarding, and they learn something new about customer value and customer decision making. Sometimes they find to their utter surprise that they have been chronically underpricing, and that establishing a much more progressive pricing regime can help them gain access to premium customers and start to grow quickly and sustainably.

Even without doing the actual price doubling experiment in the market, thinking about what would be required to support such a price point is a valuable exercise in customer centric thinking and can lead to breakthroughs on how to reposition the value being delivered by a company.

Companies have done these two exercises and increased their prices by 100%, even 300%. Other companies have decided that 5%, or 25% or 50% increases are more suitable for their circumstances. In any case, their financial viability and ability to reinvest has been improved by gaining insight.

The next sections of the book then started to explore other techniques and approaches that companies use to help achieve a more satisfactory business outcome. Many companies, particularly those making consumer goods, use cognitive biases such as framing and priming to achieve certain market outcomes. Once the correct perspective is acquired, it's easy to see that customers, particularly consumers, are often quite irrational. Looking at some of the more interesting cognitive biases, these can be employed by high-growth companies either to improve the customer experience, or nudge customers towards decisions that will be in their own interest. Some techniques such as using multiple price point options in order to help direct customers' decision making are surprisingly common. The use of framing and priming is a legitimate way to be more competitive in the marketplace and deliver greater customer value to boot.

The content in the book up to this stage will have already helped many to review their own pricing decisions and conclude what changes may be necessary, or what experiments need to be carried out in the market to make sensible adjustments. The next chapter added to this by offering some natural extensions of the content into further suggested strategies on how companies set or increase prices effectively.

Brand has an important role to play in the perception and value delivery of many products, and brand, along with packaging, is one of the few differentiating factors in thousands of product categories. Sometimes covert means are used by companies to disguise real prices, and initial prices can be very different to the real prices that the customer ends up paying. Either the customer never notices, or by the time they find out it's too late for them to change their path. Similarly, some customers have *hot buttons* that are best avoided. One such case for many consultancy and service companies are the day rates that the service charges. Sometimes, companies have found reducing a day rate is seen by a customer as being very favourable, even if the average number of days over the relationship increases, making the total sale value unchanged.

Many customers like to be able to decide how much to pay. Offering a pricing menu to these customers gives them this option. The extent to which the products are different, or actually not very different at all, is encompassed in the design of the range, and there appears to be a wide variety of approaches taken by different companies. Some sectors establish multiple price points for very similar products in order to provide framing for purchase decisions. Similarly, once a customer is engaged, offering upsell and on-sell options can be a mutually rewarding source of value.

Different classes of clients have differing needs, and although perhaps convenient, it's not rational to treat them all the same with regard to price. Therefore, companies use pricing to reflect their diversity in the same way as a traditional market segmentation, with some customers willing, able and prepared to pay more, others perhaps to pay less. It goes without saying that, all things being equal, those customers who prefer to pay more are usually the more attractive partners in these commercial interactions, providing the economic surpluses required for reinvestment and all the good things which follow.

As well as differing classes of behaviour, customer behaviour can vary over time. Depending on the 'stickiness' of a particular relationship, many suppliers raise their prices for individual customers over time. These pricing runways raise prices at a rate unlikely to stimulate a negative response from the engaged sticky customer. The starting point for these pricing runways can, of course, also be different for different customers.

CONTINUOUS VALUE MANAGEMENT

Fundamentally, if there's a central tenet to smart pricing, it's to revisit price *often*. One of the key lessons from studying how companies set price is the realisation of how important it is and yet how infrequently it's reviewed. Being so crucial means that any business should keep it 'front and centre' amongst the various things that it concerns itself with.

For larger corporations, we saw in Chapter 1 examples where losses could have been avoided by very small increases in average transaction value – as low as a few percentage points. We asked the question of whether it was reasonable to think that the board of directors and senior managers couldn't find a way to implement such a rise? It's possible that many large corporations and their boards of directors don't revisit the role of pricing frequently enough and instead see it as a periodic task to be delegated. This is perhaps because price is not regarded as something progressive, something to be actively managed, reviewed and controlled. Or perhaps it's seen as just far too complex, with too many products. Directors probably delegate the responsibility to mid-level management, even though price's influence and potential should qualify it as a matter of the utmost importance.

One single but very useful top-level question that could be tabled at every meeting of the board of directors is as follows:

1. *What was the date of the last pricing change across each of our products?*

Often, pricing is visited infrequently, or sometimes only once. There's often some emotional baggage associated with setting prices, and this may go some way in explaining why it is that people either feel awkward or fearful when undertaking this task. Also, the sheer quantity of price points in a larger organisation may make answering specific questions too time consuming for the board room. However, this simple question may be enough to prevent price stagnation and some of the other problems we've encountered, as well as to have a dramatic effect on the use of pricing in achieving favourable business outcomes.

For the more progressive, or more 'hands on' board of directors, there are another two questions that could be usefully broached:

2. *What are our price levels compared to those others offered in the market?*

Who inhabits which price point? In which way are these points lower, equal or higher than others? What are the resulting pricing signals being given to the market? These are all useful questions to revisit time and again. In some markets, prices are continuously and dynamically adjusted, so speed of change can vary tremendously. This question, in tandem with Question 1 can help directors and managers explain, discuss and review relative pricing strategies.

3. *What are the reference points that our customers use to make pricing value judgements?*

We've seen that customers are often unable to bring to bear any form of independently calibrated measure of how much something should cost. Instead, they use convenient reference points to try and establish what is good or poor value. This can include competitor pricing, but also the 'pricing menu' from a given supplier, the 'journey' of price discovery, the price environment, and any other external reference points.

These three simple questions could elevate the topic of pricing to the level of exposure it deserves, and I would argue that pricing should be a standing item on any commercial board agenda.

BENCHMARKING GROSS MARGINS

One way of analysing whether you are making the most of pricing-driven opportunities is to actively look at community benchmarks, such as analysing and comparing gross margins against other market participants.

Gross margins are the selling price of a product minus the cost of sales,[2] which is an accounting term for the more direct, or more variable, types of cost. To illustrate this, imagine a company with two locations, one head office and one factory. The head office sells products which are manufactured and then shipped out to customers from the factory. All of the costs incurred in the factory to make the product ready to ship would be included as a cost of sales. This includes the raw materials used to manufacture the product, the factory labour used in the production process, plus a portion of other factory costs including machinery costs, building costs, energy costs and so on. By contrast, the costs of the head office are not included in the cost of sales (they would be reported further down in the P&L or income statement).

The sales price minus the cost of sales gives the gross profit. This is called the gross margin when it's expressed as a percentage of the selling price. If you sell something for £100 and have a cost of sales of £30 (the cost for the factory to produce it ready for shipment) then you have a gross profit of £70, and a gross margin of 70%. This margin can then be compared with other companies, and industry averages, offering important insights.

Selling price	£100
– Cost of sales	£30
= Gross profit	£70
Gross margin	*70%*

Different industries tend to have different typical gross margins. Therefore, you can benchmark your margins against other companies in the same sector to discover whether you are at the higher or lower end of the spectrum. Many online databases show gross margins for specific companies or industries, whilst Companies House in the UK offers a free service to inspect the financial accounts filed by any UK company.

Some industries have gross margins of 70%, others 90%, yet others 40%. This difference is usually due to the structural features of the sector – the relationship between unit sales and the more variable element of costs – and is fairly consistent within a given sector. Therefore, it's important to know what your industry averages are, and it can be a useful indicator of whether your price is high or low in your particular sector.

Some examples can be seen below:

	Engineering	Software	Furniture Making
Sales	100	100	100
Cost of Sales	65	1	61
Gross margin	*35%*	*99%*	*39%*

iPhone gross margins were reportedly between 60% and 74% between 2007 and 2018[3] – in other words, the manufacturing cost of the device was 26% to 40% of the selling price over the period. Coffee is a physical product that has notoriously high gross margins, often 80%, even in a service setting – one reason that coffee shops can be so successful.[4] To benchmark your own business there are many resources available online to help.[5]

BEAUTY IS IN THE EYE OF THE CUSTOMER

It's important to remember to retain some humility in the face of the customer. Analysis can be very powerful, but we must accept that analysis can be wrong. This can be because of flaws in the analysis (think back to the market research test in the New Coke example), or because the market is far more nuanced and complex than can be easily understood, or simply that customers are happily irrational – and there's nothing wrong with this, as long as we accept its possibility.

The long-standing expression 'the customer is always right' is an interesting one. Sometimes it's correct, at other times it's not. There's therefore a balance between helping direct customers to the decisions they make, and actively listening to customers. Hence the importance of trying new things and using market experiments and measurementto overcome complexity in customer decision making.

USING MARKET EXPERIMENTS

Growing a business can be hard. And managing a business can sometimes feel as if there are more unknowns and uncertainties than there are things known. There's a considerable body of business theory and analysis tools available to help cope with large amounts of complexity and data to help with the uncertainty. However, sooner or later we run out of reliable reference points to make sensible decisions.

We have many thousands of libraries in business schools across the world filled with a collective knowledge of how business 'works'. And yet there are many surprises: Each year many businesses unexpectedly go bust, sometimes leaving behind thousands of employees in dire straits. Every few years entirely new categories of markets appear which are revolutionary and grow unexpectedly, changing the nature of our modern world for the better or worse.

Despite our confidence in what we know, there's usually more that we don't fully understand. We therefore have a bounded rationality. This rationality is limited by what we know and what is effective to gather and analyse.

There's an apocryphal story about a group of venture scouts who are lost in the Alps during a snowstorm. There's a good chance they will perish. Then, someone finds a map in their pocket, and using the map they find their way to safety, to everyone's relief. Then, the next day, they look at the map again and realise it's for a completely different part of the Alps, and not at all for the valley they were in. The apparent lesson is that sometimes any strategy, any information, is better than none, especially if it helps bring structure to the chaos. Similarly, businesspeople sometimes grasp whatever information they can in order to try and make decisions. So, whilst it's important to have great humility when it comes to pleasing customers, be aware that making introspective decisions can be limited in value.

Is there a better way? I think there is a much underused approach related to running market experiments. A suggested method to carrying this out is in the exercise in Chapter 7. When we don't know the answer to something, why not use the market to give us the answer? When we don't know what a new product should be, why not conduct an experiment to find the answer?

Instead of launching one version of a product, why not launch several, measure the relative results and see which the market prefers? Instead of launching one price point, why not try several in several different geographies at the same time and see which outperforms the others? Trying new things, establishing new price points, finding different ways to frame value with different reference points, these are a few examples of ways of conducting experiments in the market, where the results can be measured and can give meaningful insights to customer decision making. This experimental approach, using the market mechanism of actual customer purchase decisions, overcomes many of the problems associated with traditional research.

ON THE ROAD TO SUCCESS

Although not directly related to smart pricing, I've listed below some additional observations on good practices for high-growth early stage businesses, which are also valid for new innovative product introductions for larger companies: start-ups and early stage businesses have some special requirements, but many of these principles are true for larger organisations too. These are therefore some general tips and advice for any organisation with aspirations for growth.

The early hurdles of setting up a new business are well defined: choose a name, incorporate a legal entity, raise capital, develop a product or service to sell, negotiate key partnerships and so on. For larger corporations launching a new product, market research is usually followed by product development, then approval is sought, then products are manufactured and then sent out to the channels. In each case, having made all of this effort, it's a shame that the failure rate is so high. It's said that up to 90% of technology start-ups or new product introductions fail. They either fail outright, or never achieve the anticipated results. Whilst some of these failures may have been inevitable, many are due to common errors that undermine a company's ability to survive, grow and scale.[6] Please therefore find below the 'top 5' most common tips for success that I use when mentoring and supporting early stage companies:

#1. CONSTANTLY STRIVE FOR SMART PRICING

For early stage companies already active in the marketplace, and already profitable, an unsustainably low price is perhaps the most common error limiting growth. The negative consequences of this error are that the business is never able to produce the cash margin it requires (and deserves) to reinvest, and either growth is stifled or even survival threatened. As you know now, price has a disproportionately large effect on a business. This book has covered the usual reasons for underpricing and what to do about it.

#2. IT'S MUCH EASIER TO SELL SOMETHING CUSTOMERS WANT

An *easy sell product* is one that a customer sees, instantly understands and immediately wants. By contrast, unfortunately, many products have the opposite attributes: they are hard to get in front of a customer, they need significant investment in explanations before the customer will even be in a position to decide whether they like it or not, and then, finally, customer responses to the value proposition are lukewarm.

For high-growth companies of all sizes, these combined issues probably pose the biggest problem when developing and launching an innovative new product. This is particularly true for technology companies since their highly innovative products are often in brand new categories, which sometimes have never existed before, and therefore there's no established buying behaviour for them. In this situation, innovative companies literally don't know what they don't know.

Instead of embracing this conundrum, companies often assume that a ready market exists for a new product or service, and assume they know how this should be developed and delivered. Once these assumptions become embedded it can be very difficult to shift them. This overconfidence error often manifests itself as a product or service that is very difficult to actually sell.

I like to call this a high-burden sale and it tends to have a characteristic of either

   a. Having high customer educational requirements, or
   b. Seeking to fix a problem that's causing a low level of 'pain'[7]

High educational requirements mean a seller has to invest a lot of time and/or money to explain to the customer what the value proposition is. If, at the end of this, the conversion rate and gross margins aren't high enough, the seller will go out of business. Low-pain fixing products are 'nice to haves' that no one in today's busy world can actually be bothered to get around to buying. The apocryphal *product graveyard* is crammed full of the 'better mouse traps' that nobody bought. Refer back to Chapter 8 for more on customer decision making.

Techniques such as The Lean Start-up methodology help avoid these risks. Essentially, they acknowledge the lack of certainty in the system and take an incremental approach with strategic sales interactions to discover a product that customers will actually really care about and buy. The approach is based on market experiments and simulating or getting as close as possible to genuine purchasing behaviour – which can be far more reliable than traditional market research.

#3 HIRE A COMPETENT SECOND-IN-CHARGE EARLY ON

When new businesses are established, there is often a single founder. As the first member of staff, this founder must do all the tasks of the business, since there is no one else. As the business grows more staff are recruited, but sometimes the founder role remains at the centre of all decision making – the 'hub' with many spokes running out from this. In organisational theory this company culture is sometimes called a club model with centralised decision-making resting with one person.

The problem with this model is that it will not scale very well. As a business grows someone needs to take a view of the big picture and take a strategic view. This is difficult to do when entrenched in high levels of detail and 'firefighting' whatever problem is being tackled at that point in time. By contrast, scalable businesses have recruited a trusted 'second in charge' – someone with similar intellectual capabilities as the founder, who is able to take the 'day to day' tasks away from the founder, allowing them to step back and see the big picture. This is also sometimes called 'spending time *on* your business, not *in* your business'. This enables businesses to be strategic and to scale and grow.

#4 VERIFY A SCALABLE BUSINESS MODEL BEFORE ACTUALLY SCALING UP

Not doing this is an error that normally leads to a business running out of cash. Many early stage businesses have high cash burn rates. They are losing money, burning through a certain amount of their cash reserves each month. This is fine as long as it's planned for, and key growth objectives are being achieved whilst the company burns through its cash. However, the key issue is whether those achievements are actually leading the company to become cash break-even as planned for, or not.

In some cases, companies have not solved the key challenges they face with regards to gaining and exploiting new business, or whatever the key objectives are whilst they are burning cash – it may not be sales: for tech start-ups it may be R&D success, which in turn leads to a trade sale of the business itself.

For example, a new company may have gained some initial sales and then, buoyed by this success, starts to recruit heavily, takes up new offices and adds more and more cost, increasing the monthly burn rate. This is usually done in the expectation that sales will follow. However, if the major 'unknowns' have not been explored, if the business model is not truly understood, then the business will stutter, further sales will not be forth-coming and the high burn rate will send the company into failure.

Instead, before increasing the overhead expenditure, a company should be sure that it has fully explored its business model and can be confident that sales growth (or whatever the objective is) will follow. I sometimes use the analogy of a hand-cranked music box. Building the music box, with all of its components, and ensuring it plays the correct tune is the initial phase of start-up exploration and finding a sustainable business model. Once the music box is working well, then the next phase is to start turning the handle faster and faster, making the music faster and louder – this is successful scaling up, where more expenditure can be made with confidence.

There is also a separate and specific cash management issue related to working capital, as we covered in Chapter 5. Even if very profitable, if a company has a starkly negative working capital model, then growth will inevitably place high demands on cash, and these cash needs have to be met to avoid insolvency.

#5 IN THE FACE OF UNCERTAINTY, USE INCREMENTAL STEPS

I've already mentioned the power of using market experiments to guide key decision making. Market analysis and business theory can be very power-ful, but customer decision making can be complex, or even, to an outside observer, irrational.

An alternative approach to using traditional market research to make sense of the world is to use the market mechanism to provide insights – this can be achieved by setting market experiments and making incremental adjustments to business decisions. This is a key principle in engineering science: make a change and then measure the effect of that change. If it's a positive step forward, integrate this change and move forward with another incremental change. If it's a negative result, revert to the previous state and try another direction.

A key principle of this approach is the *measurement of the resulting change.* This establishes a feedback loop for informed decision making, based on actual changes in customer behaviour. These market tests are sometimes called touch and learn cycles.

Establishing and using such feedback loops can be a very powerful technique for incisive decision making – sometimes vital for growth businesses in competitive environments.

FINALLY

Thank you for taking the time to read this book. I've certainly enjoyed writing it and I hope you've found reading it as much fun as I have had writing it down.

If you want to know more, some great materials written by others are listed in the Appendices.

I hope you've enjoyed the journey and have found it valuable. Please keep in touch and let me know how you get on with your own business at www.DoubleYourPrice.com

D.A.M.F.

NOTES

CHAPTER 1

1. https://ustr.gov/trade-agreements/free-trade-agreements/
transatlantic-trade-and-investment-partnership-t-tip/t-tip-12

2. I predominantly use 'product' throughout the book, but please read
this as 'product or service'.

CHAPTER 2

1. See https://dcincubator.co.uk/blog/60-of-new-businesses-fail-in-the-
first-3-years-heres-why/

2. In negotiations theory and practice this question is valid equally for
both customers and suppliers to help understand their underlying
motivations.

3. See https://www.innocentdrinks.co.uk/content/dam/innocent/gb/en/
files/innocent-good-all-round-report-2019.pdf

4. See William A Sahlman: *Innocent Drinks,* Harvard Business School,
2004.

5. See William A Sahlman: *Innocent Drinks,* Harvard Business School, 2004.

6. See https://www.marketingweek.com/consumers-regard-for-
innocent-crashes/

7. See https://www.trustedreviews.com/news/android-phones-nearly-
three-times-cheaper-than-iphone-2924886

8. See https://www.digitaltrends.com/web/amazon-more-expensive-
that-competition-when-it-comes-to-most-books/

9. See https://en.wikipedia.org/wiki/Tesco#UK_operations

10. See https://www.mirror.co.uk/money/tesco-cost-up-11-more-13340632

CHAPTER 3

1. This represents a net income loss of £163m against sales of
£9584m. See https://www.morningstar.com/stocks/chix/tcgl/
financials

2. This represents a 2013 gross profit loss of £887k against sales of £675m and a 2014 gross profit loss of £5629k against sales of £668m. Calculations based on Companies House figures. See https://find-and-update.company-information.service.gov.uk/company/NF001705/filing-history and https://www.figurewizard.com/BHS-Profit.html

CHAPTER 4

1. The 4 Ps are Price, Place, Promotion and Product https://www.investopedia.com/terms/f/four-ps.asp

2. By contrast, the recent emergence of the field of behavioural economics is helping give companies a new understanding of customer behaviour and decision making.

3. More broadly, supply and demand curves meet at a price which clears the market.

4. Also, please note that for all these charts, the prices are from the same retailer to give a fair and valid comparison.

5. https://www.theguardian.com/business/2015/dec/14/nurofens-maker-admits-misleading-consumers-over-contents-in-painkillers

6. https://www.ukmeds.co.uk/nytol-one-a-night

7. https://www.medicines.org.uk/emc/product/8071/pil

8. https://www.chemist-4-u.com/antihistamine-cream-25g

9. Porter, Michael E., *Competitive Advantage: Creating and Sustaining Superior Performance,* Free Press, 2004.

10. Michael Porter's work actually analyses differentiation strategies and cost leadership strategies in the context of either industry-wide or focused segment activities. If a company tries differentiation, cost leadership and focus strategies all together, they will be 'stuck in the middle'. However, the simplified approach of 'cost versus differentiation' used here fits our uncomplicated needs better.

11. https://www.wsj.com/graphics/apple-cash/

12. Another reason can be taxation differences in different countries, especially for alcohol and luxury goods.

13. Prospecting theory from economics also describes how individuals assess their loss and gain perspectives in an asymmetric manner – losses are more keenly felt than the equivalent gain.

CHAPTER 5

1. Marn, Michael V. and Rosiello, Robert L., 'Managing price, gaining profit', *Harvard Business Review,* Sept–Oct 1992.

2. This will, of course, be true 50% of the time given the nature of an average.

3. https://www.mckinsey.com/business-functions/marketing-and-sales/our-insights/pricing-distributors-most-powerful-value-creation-lever

4. https://thealchemist.uk.com/

CHAPTER 6

1. Actually, their profit is dictated by the difference between the price they paid to buy the car (which they keep secret) and the sale price they achieve in reselling it.

2. e.g. Financial data from the past, not historical figures such as Henry VIII!

3. https://en.wikipedia.org/wiki/Satisficing

4. https://www.seedlipdrinks.com/en-gb/our-story/

5. https://www.gov.uk/tax-on-shopping/alcohol-tobacco

6. Chartered Institute of Marketing; Help to Grow, HM Government, Small Business Charter

7. Almquist, Eric, Senior, John and Bloch, Nicolas, 'The elements of value', *Harvard Business Review,* Sept 2016. https://hbr.org/2016/09/the-elements-of-value and https://media.bain.com/elements-of-value/

8. Almquist, Eric, Senior, John and Bloch, Nicolas, 'The elements of value', *Harvard Business Review,* Sept 2016. https://hbr.org/2016/09/the-elements-of-value and https://media.bain.com/elements-of-value/

9. An opportunity cost is the loss of value caused by not pursuing a given course of action https://en.wikipedia.org/wiki/Opportunity_cost

CHAPTER 7

1. Steenkamp, Jan-Benedict E.M., 'The relationship between price and quality in the marketplace', *De Economist,* 136, 491–507, 1988.

2. Yun Jae, Hwang, Roe, Brian E. and Teisl M.F., 'Does price signal quality? Strategic implications of price as a signal of quality for the

case of genetically modified food'. *International Food and Agribusiness Management Review,* 9, 93–114, 2006.

3. Verma, D.P.S. and Sen Gupta, Soma, 'Does higher price signal better quality?' *Vikalpa,* 29(2), 2004.

4. Gerstner, Eitan, 'Do high prices signal higher quality?' *Journal of Marketing Research,* 22(2), 209–215, 1985.

5. https://www.psychologytoday.com/gb/blog/the-science-behind-behavior/201802/when-high-prices-attract-consumers-and-low-prices-repel-them

6. The psychology of pricing, Shapiro, Benson P, Harvard Business Review, 1968.

7. https://www.pnas.org/doi/10.1073/pnas.0706929105

8. Deval, Hélène, Mantel, Susan P., Kardes, Frank R. and Posavac, Steven S., 'High quality or poor value: When do consumers make different conclusions about the same product?' *Journal of Consumer Research,* 2012. https://www.sciencedaily.com/releases/2012/10/121022121908.htm

9. https://hbr.org/2017/10/why-you-should-charge-clients-more-than-you-think-youre-worth

10. https://www.adbrands.net/archive/uk/stella-artois-uk-p.htm

11. https://en.wikipedia.org/wiki/Reassuringly_Expensive

12. https://hbr.org/2012/09/bringing-science-to-the-art-of-strategy

13. Plassman, Hilke, O'Doherty, John, Shiv, Baba and Rangel, Antonio, 'Marketing actions can modulate neural representations of experienced pleasantness'. *Proceedings of the National Academy of Science,* 105(3), 1050–1054, 2008; https://doi.org/10.1073/pnas.0706929105. https://www.pnas.org/content/105/3/1050.full

14. https://www.hkstrategies.com/en/magnify-neuromarketing-its-all-in-your-head/

15. https://en.wikipedia.org/wiki/Coca-Cola

16. https://en.wikipedia.org/wiki/Judgment_of_Paris_(wine)

17. Kahneman, Daniel, *Thinking, Fast and Slow,* Penguin, 2012.

18. https://hbr.org/2015/04/why-strong-customer-relationships-trump-powerful-brands

19. https://hbr.org/2015/04/why-strong-customer-relationships-trump-powerful-brands

20. In fact, the unusual position of holding onto the cash rather than paying it out is partly due to the tax treatment of those funds and Apple perhaps waiting for a better tax regime in order to repatriate these funds and return some of them to shareholders.

CHAPTER 8

1. https://www.inc.com/inc5000/
2. Teece, David, Pisano, Gary and Shuen, Amy, *Firm Capabilities, Resources, and the Concept of Strategy.* University of California, Berkeley: Center for Research on Management, 1990.

CHAPTER 10

1. Kahneman, Daniel, *Thinking, Fast and Slow,* Penguin, 2012.
2. Graves, Philips, *Consumer.ology,* Nicholas Brealey, 2010.
3. Kahneman, Daniel, *Thinking, Fast and Slow,* Penguin, 2012.
4. Tversky and Kahneman. https://en.wikipedia.org/wiki/Framing_(social_sciences)#Experimental_demonstration
5. https://en.wikipedia.org/wiki/Framing_(social_sciences)#Experimental_demonstration
6. Expected number theory says, on average, if someone was able to make investments such as this, it would yield a return of 150%, or an impressive 50% net gain over the invested amount.
7. There is no perfect answer as to the question of 'Should I make the first offer?' However, my attempt at an answer is that having carried out all of your preparation for a negotiation and reviewed all of the available information (such as looking at alternative) you believe that you have superior information over the other party, then it might be in your favour to make the first offer and anchor the negotiation. However, if you believe the other party has superior information, then it might be in your favour to wait for them to make the first offer – you might be surprised by its level.
8. https://www.fastfoodmenuprices.com/starbucks-prices/
9. https://www.natso.com/topics/with-coffee-cup-size-live-large
10. Dan Ariely https://www.youtube.com/watch?v=xOhb4LwAaJk&feature=emb_logo

CHAPTER 11

1. https://www.lightspeedhq.co.uk/blog/why-do-restaurants-fail/

2. https://www.fca.org.uk/publication/discussion/dp18-09.pdf

3. https://www.forbes.com/powerful-brands/list/

4. The option to buy the software outright tends to come and go. Sometimes the option is available to certain types of customer groups only. There's a clear preference evident in the pricing for subscription models.

5. https://www.theguardian.com/money/2013/sep/07/switching-banks-seven-day

6. N. B. If you are under 50 and think these development cost numbers sound crazy, you are right, but in the year 2000 building a web business meant designing and building much of the front, middle and back office code virtually from scratch. Something which might take half a day now with the tools available today might have taken a programmer three months to do back in 2000. Furthermore, few people knew how to build websites and there was a great scarcity of resources.

7. Dubner, Stephen J. and Levitt, Steven D., *Freakonomics,* William Morrow and Company, 2005.

CHAPTER 12

1. https://en.wikipedia.org/wiki/List_of_mergers_and_acquisitions_by_Apple

2. Or 'cost of goods sold' in the USA

3. https://www.phonearena.com/news/Profit-margins-on-the-iPhone-have-fallen-to-60_id111023

4. https://godigitally.io/food-vs-coffee-gross-profit-margin/

5. One example resource for US companies can be found at https://www.readyratios.com/sec/ratio/gross-margin/

6. 'What's the difference between grow and scale?' I hear you say. Although sometime used as synonyms, I like to think of growing as increasing in size through a wide variety of techniques including R&D, innovating and launching new products. By contrast, scaling is doing more of what you already do.

7. For further information on this idea of problem 'pain' see *The Lean Start-up,* Eric Ries.

THE SMART PRICING SUMMARY WORKBOOK

INTRODUCTION

In this book we've seen how underpricing is the #1 error with innovative businesses. Innovation poses some special challenges due to a lack of exemplars or established norms. Not only for small or new businesses, large corporations too make critical errors about the importance of price setting. Instead, the convenient focus for the entrepreneur or the manager tends to be on top-line growth without considering the sustainability of operations and the all-important dynamic of generating cash for reinvestment.

CHAPTER 2

In Chapter 2, we saw some of the reasons companies tell themselves for not being able to raise prices, the role of cognitive biases in their management thinking, and how actually, most successful growth businesses charge a relatively premium price for their products. The most visible consequence of not charging a high enough price is the lack of funds to pay the staff well, but the more serious implication is a lack of funds to reinvest in product development and to support growing cash flow requirements.

Underpricing
If you suspect you are underpricing, why do you think you are doing this?

e.g. lack of confidence, fear of insufficient sales, price is immutable

Cognitive bias
Which cognitive biases are you subject to?

e.g. confirmation bias, anchoring, availability bias

Interests
In whose interests are your buyers acting?

What are those interests?

CHAPTER EXERCISE

Whose interests are being represented? (Page 11)

CHAPTER 3

In Chapter 3 we reviewed the relationship between price and value. We saw that it's not only early-stage businesses that fail to spend enough time on pricing, larger corporations too make the same error. Some examples highlighted that a small increase in price, or average transaction value, would have meant reaching break-even for several recent high-profile corporate collapses.

'Soul' insights

Which company would you prefer to have?
a. A £100m sales company with profits of £1m? Why? / Why not?
or
b. A £10m sales company with profits of £1m? Why? / Why not?

Potential?

Which companies (or brands) that you interact with do you think have growth potential? What role does price have in this?

CHAPTER 4

Next, we reviewed traditional pricing theory and how, as consumers, we have been programmed to accept certain rules and concepts, usually without asking about the underlying logic. We saw that many functionally identical products are sold at multiple price points and, actually, some products are routinely sold at price points three to ten times the price of their peers – despite being essentially identical. This result alone should excite the entrepreneurially spirited – a 'door opening' to new and sophisticated opportunities for differentiation and profitability. We also saw that companies (usually) can't be the cheapest and the best and still expect to make money.

Product life cycle

Where in the product life cycle are your products, and what does this suggest in terms of price and competitive pressures?

Price or differentiation leader?

Which one are you? Or, are you stuck in the middle? (If so, how can you correct this?)

Pricing scattergram

Where do your products sit in the landscape of competitive offerings? Can you see opportunities with unfulfilled niches?

Pricing methods

Do you use cost plus, competitor-based or value-based pricing?

Is this the most effective method, and if so, why/why not?

CHAPTER EXERCISE

Produce your own pricing scattergram (Page 46)

CHAPTER 5

In Chapter 5, we defined what growth means in the context of a high-growth business and considered research from *Harvard Business Review* that measured the huge influence price has on profits. It highlighted that a change in price has almost four times the effect on profits that the same change in revenues has. Research from McKinsey also suggested nonlinear relationships that some companies take advantage of when they actively price – with big differences in the level of scrutiny given to prices by customers across different categories of product.

As we saw with our generic Company A and B example, it's perfectly possible to have a higher price and lose some potential customers, to convert less leads into sales than would be the case with a lower price, and yet still have a much more profitable enterprise. Such an enterprise is able to reinvest in important strategic areas and therefore grow well. We also looked at working capital, explained why some business 'go bust' by increasing their sales rapidly, and the role of pricing to avoid that.

> **Price leverage**
> Work out your price leverage *x*%
> Is this higher or lower than your competitors?

> **Working capital**
> Do you have a positive or negative working capital cycle?
> How does this affect your cash requirements for growth in the future?

CHAPTER EXERCISE

Working out your price leverage (Page 68)

CHAPTER 6

We then moved on to challenge the validity of 'cost plus' pricing strategies for high-growth businesses. Despite its enduring popularity, 'cost plus' does not meet any of the key demands of a well-differentiated product in a modern economy. It can also detrimentally shift the focus of the company's offering from the customer's perspective to the one of internal operations.

Instead, we looked at how value-based pricing seeks to understand what value actually means to the customer and use this information to set the price. Within this context of understanding value, we also looked at the importance of customer reference points, bundling products together and the importance of adding emotional value. We also looked at some ways that destructive price competition is avoided by some sectors, whilst simultaneously pulling off the trick of increasing customer perceived value.

Value 'pie'
Are your interactions integrative or distributive?
In what way?
If integrative, how can you increase the overall value pie?
If distributive, how can you claim a larger slice?

Value-based pricing
Carry out the value-based pricing exercise.
How does this compare with your current pricing decisions and strategy?

Unprofitable customers?
Which of your customers are unprofitable?
How might you be able to 'let them go'?

CHAPTER EXERCISE

Using value-based pricing (Page 88)

CHAPTER 7

Chapter 7 is one of the most important chapters: it highlights research using brain scans which seems to prove that all things being equal, people actually feel more physically rewarding when they pay more. Previous studies of similar products being sold at vastly different price points had indicated that price has a strong influence on how customers perceive quality and how they judge the value derived from a product. But the brain scans actually show that this counter-intuitive result is physically represented in the brain. The reward centres in subjects' brains are energised by a high price point irrespective of whether the product is different or not. This important result goes some way to help us reset our own assumptions about our own rationality, that of our customers', as well as about our approaches to setting price.

> **Challenging price points**
> In what progressive and useful ways can you challenge price points by changing your assumptions?
> What have you discovered about customer value recognition?
> What experiments can you run to make more discoveries?

> **What don't you yet know?**
> What aspects of sales and pricing in your business do you not yet fully understand, but would save you time and/or money to know before scaling up existing processes?
> How can you run experiments to find the answers?

CHAPTER EXERCISE

Design a market experiment (Page 113)

CHAPTER 8

Chapter 8 explained the mechanism by which reinvesting profits back into a high-growth business can generate large financial returns. Often, the internal rate of return of a high-growth company or innovative project is 25% to 50%. Every pound that is reinvested will grow at that compound rate each and every year to follow. Comparing this reinvestment dynamic with a company that has lower prices and simply pays out dividends shows the very different outcomes, even after just a few years.

> **Market**
> Is your product in an existing category or creating new category with new buying behaviour?
> In what way?

> **USP**
> For every segment you serve:
> 1. What value or benefit are you offering?
> 2. What makes you unique and better than the competition?
> 3. Why will someone buy from you? What's your USP?

CHAPTER EXERCISE

Doing the USP analysis (Page 140)

CHAPTER 9

In this chapter a challenge was set. Can you double your price? Or, more accurately, are there safe tests you can carry out in the market to see what happens if you double your price? The question also posed was 'What do you need to do to justify this price increase?' Many companies have tried this test and often found the exercise very rewarding, learning something new about customer value and customer decision making. Sometimes, they found to their utter surprise that they have been chronically underpricing, and establishing a much more progressive pricing regime can help them gain access to premium customers and start to grow quickly and sustainably.

Even without doing the actual price-doubling experiment in the market, thinking about what would be required to support such a price point is a valuable exercise in customer-centric thinking and can lead to break-throughs on how to reposition the value being delivered by a company. Some companies have done these exercises and increased their prices by 100%, even 300%. Other companies have decided that 5% to 50% increase is more suitable for their circumstances, which are nonetheless significant for their ability to thrive and grow.

Double your price Is there a safe way to test what happens if you double your price? *e.g. entering a new market, launching a new product, creating a parallel product*	**Customer decision making** How do customers weigh up decisions? Map their decision-making process. *e.g. effort, time, money, emotions, loyalty, distraction*

CHAPTER EXERCISE

1. *Double your price* (Page 148)

2. *Map the customer decision-making process* (Page 156)

CHAPTER 10

This chapter explored other techniques and approaches that companies use to help achieve a more satisfactory business outcome. Many companies, particularly those making consumer goods, use cognitive biases such as framing and priming in order to achieve certain market outcomes.

Once the correct perspective is acquired, it's easy to see that customers, particularly consumers, are often quite irrational. Looking at some of the more interesting cognitive biases, these can be employed by high-growth companies to either improve the customer experience or lead customers to decisions that will be in their own interest. Some techniques, such as using multiple price point options in order to help direct customers' decision making, are surprisingly common. The use of framing and priming is a legitimate way to be more competitive in the marketplace and deliver greater customer value too.

> **Embracing biases**
> What customer biases are you aware of?
> In what way do competitors use biases to add or remove customer value?

CHAPTER EXERCISE

Identify biases in your own organisation (Page 170)

CHAPTER 11

The content in the book to this stage will have already helped many to review their own pricing decisions and conclude what changes may be necessary, or what experiments need to be carried out in the market in order to make sensible adjustments. This chapter built upon this by offering some natural extensions to the content of additional suggested strategies on how to increase prices effectively.

Brand has an important role to play in the perception and value delivery of many products, and brand, along with packaging, is one of the few differentiating factors among thousands of product categories.

Sometimes covert means are used by companies to disguise real prices, and these can be very different to the real prices that the customer ends up paying. Either the customer never notices, or by the time they find out it's too late for them to change their path. Similarly, some customers have 'hot buttons' that are best avoided. One such case for many consultancy and service companies is the day rate that the service provider charges. Sometimes reducing a day rate is seen as being very favourable by a customer, even if the average number of days over the relationship increases, making the total sale value unchanged.

Many customers like to be able to decide how much to pay. Offering a pricing menu to these customers gives them this option. The extent to which the products on the menu are different, or actually not very different at all, is up to the supplier, and there appears to be a wide variety of approaches taken by different companies. Some sectors establish multiple price points for very similar products in order to provide framing for purchase decisions. Similarly, once a customer is engaged, offering upsell and on-sell options can be a mutually rewarding source of value.

Different classes of clients have differing needs, and although convenient, it's not useful to treat them all the same with regard to price. Therefore, companies use pricing to reflect their diversity in the same way as a traditional market segmentation, with some customers willing, able and prepared to pay more, others perhaps to pay less. It goes without saying that, all things being equal, those customers who prefer to pay more are usually the more attractive partners in these commercial interactions, providing the economic surpluses required for reinvestment.

As well as differing classes of behaviour, customer behaviour can vary over time. Depending on the 'stickiness' of a particular relationship, many suppliers raise their prices for individual customers over time. These 'pricing runways' raise prices at a rate unlikely to stimulate a negative response from the engaged customer. The starting point for these pricing runways can, of course, also be different for differing classes of customers.

Overt or covert
Do companies in your sector use covert or overt prices increases?

Brand
What role does brand have in adding value in your industry?

Techniques used
Which techniques do companies use in your sector to raise prices?

e.g. differentiation, emotional value, pricing menus, on-selling, upselling, totals, bundling, multi-points, runways, excess demand

---

CHAPTER EXERCISE

How will you use the strategies? (Page 190)

FURTHER READING

No one work on business and management stands on its own. Instead, it relies on researchers, academics and authors. Here are some related books that I've enjoyed reading and that I can recommend:

Building an Entrepreneurial Organisation, Simon Mosey, Hannah Noke, Paul Kirkham. Routledge 2017.

Competitive Advantage: Creating and Sustaining Superior Performance, Michael E. Porter. Free Press 2004.

Confessions of the Pricing Man, Hermann Simon. Copernicus 2015.

Consumer.ology, Philip Graves. Nicholas Brealey Publishing 2013.

Contemporary Strategy Analysis, Robert M. Grant. Wiley 2019.

Extraordinary Popular Delusions and the Madness of Crowds, Charles Mackay. CreateSpace Independent Publishing Platform 2013.

Freakonomics, Stephen J. Dubner, Steven D. Levitt. Penguin 2006.

Little Bets, Peter Sims. Random House Business 2012.

Marketing Management, Philip Kotler. Pearson 2021.

Superfreakonomics, Stephen J. Dubner, Steven D. Levitt. Penguin 2010.

The Knack, How Street-Smart Entrepreneurs Learn to Handle Whatever Comes Up, Norm Brodsky and Bo Burlingham. Random House Business 2009.

The Lean Start-up: How Constant Innovation Creates Radically Successful Businesses, Eric Ries. Portfolio Penguin 2011.

Thinking, Fast and Slow, Daniel Kahneman. Penguin 2012.

APPENDIX A

COMPANY A AND B P&LS

COMPANY A AND B PROFIT AND LOSS STATEMENTS (INCOME STATEMENTS)

Company		A	B	Notes
i.	*Sales %*	*60*	*40*	sales conversion rates
ii.	*Price*	*100*	*130*	
iii.	Sales	6000	5200	i. × ii.
iv.	Variable costs @60 ea.	3600	2400	60 × i. (40%, 53% GM)
v.	Gross profit	2400	2800	iii. − iv.
vi.	Fixed cost	2000	2000	(33%, 38% of sales)
vii.	Operating profit	400	800	v. − vi. (6%, 15%)

APPENDIX B

PRICE DISCOUNTING THE AVERAGED P&L

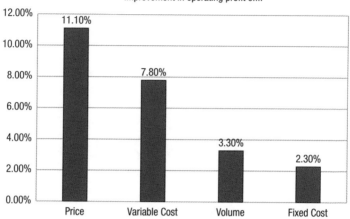

A 1% increase in each of the factors below creates an improvement in operating profit of...

We can create a P&L (or income statement) with the same characteristics as the 2,400 company average from 'Managing Price, Gaining Profit' in *Harvard Business Review*. This shows that a 1% change in price, variable cost, volume and fixed cost produces the operating profit changes reflected in the research results.

		1% changes			
	Base case	Price up	Variable cost down	Volume up	Fixed cost down
Sales	100	**101**	100	**101**	100
Variable cost	**70**	70	**69.3**	**70.7**	70
Gross profit	30	31	30.7	30.3	30
GM%	*30%*	*31%*	*31%*	*30%*	*30%*
fixed cost	**21**	21	21	21	**20.79**
Op profit	9	10	9.7	9.3	9.21
Change % to base case		*11.1%*	*7.8%*	*3.3%*	*2.3%*

Taking this average P&L, a 5% and 20% price discount can then be applied. The results to gross profit and operating profit are shown below. The increase in sales revenue required at the new price to return the profitability to the previous level is also shown.

	Base case	5% discount	To recover the discount		20% discount	To recover the discount	
Sales	100	95	*120%*	114	80	*300%*	240
Variable cost	70	70	*120%*	84	70	*300%*	210
Gross profit	30	25		30	10		30
GM%	*30%*	*26%*		*26%*	*13%*		*13%*
Fixed cost	21	21		21	21		21
Op profit	9	4		9	−11		9
% change to base case		*−55.6%*		*0.0%*	*−222.2%*		*0.0%*

INDEX